SELECTED ESSAYS ON THE ECONOMIC GROWTH OF THE SOCIALIST AND THE MIXED ECONOMY

MICHAŁ KALECKI

CAMBRIDGE
AT THE UNIVERSITY PRESS
1972

Published by the Syndics of the Cambridge University Press
Bentley House, 200 Euston Road, London NW1 2DB
American Branch: 32 East 57th Street, New York, N.Y.10022

Library of Congress Catalogue Card Number: 73-179162

ISBN: 0 521 08447 4

Printed in Great Britain
at the University Printing House, Cambridge
(Brooke Crutchley, University Printer)

SELECTED ESSAYS ON
THE ECONOMIC GROWTH OF
THE SOCIALIST AND THE
MIXED ECONOMY

CONTENTS

v

Contents

PUBLISHER'S NOTE

This book completes Kalecki's selected essays and is the sequel to *Selected Essays on the Dynamics of the Capitalist Economy* (1971). Although Michał Kalecki died without having written his introduction for this book, the choice of essays for inclusion was entirely his.

Part I was published in Polish in 1963; the English translation, by Zdzisław Sadowski, was first published by Basil Blackwell in 1969. The appendix to part I is an excerpt from the paper contributed to *Socialism, Capitalism and Economic Growth: essays presented to Maurice Dobb*, Cambridge University Press, 1967. Chapter 12 was published, in Polish, in a Festschrift for A. Wakar, *Problemy teorii gospodarki*, Warsaw, 1970; the English translation is by D. M. Nuti. Chapter 13 was published in Russian in *Ekonomika i matematicheskiye metody*, 1970; the English translation is by D. G. Fry. Chapter 14 was published in *Introduction, Growth and Trade: Essays in Honour of Sir Roy Harrod* edited by W. A. Eltis, M. F.-G. Scott, and J. N. Wolfe, Oxford University Press, 1970. Chapter 15 was published in Polish in 1964, and subsequently in English in *Co-Existence*, 1967.

Symbols are consistent within each part, but not necessarily throughout the book.

We are grateful for the help of Dr D. M. Nuti, who has seen the book through the press.

PART I

INTRODUCTION TO THE THEORY OF GROWTH IN A SOCIALIST ECONOMY

[1963]

1. DEFINITIONS AND ASSUMPTIONS

1. Since in this essay we shall be concerned with the long-run changes in the national income and its components, we shall start from a definition of these concepts.

We define the national income in a given year as the value of goods produced in that year after deducting the value of raw materials and semi-manufactures used in the process of production. The value of imported materials is subtracted because they are not produced in the country considered; the value of home produced materials is deducted to avoid double counting. If in a given year machines are produced which require *inter alia* the production of a certain amount of steel, then by deducting the value of the steel input we avoid including the production of steel in the national income twice – first in the value of steel production, and second in that of machinery production. In this way the national income – as contrasted with the aggregate turnover – does not depend on the number of stages of production.

Inputs into the production process include not only raw materials and semi-manufactures, but also fixed capital. However, according to the definition given above, we do not deduct depreciation from the value of output and thus we are dealing with *gross* national income. This different treatment of materials on the one hand, and depreciation on the other, may seem to be inconsistent but in fact it is not. Depreciation as contrasted with the input of materials, is not a strictly determined magnitude. The life-span of productive equipment is not a purely technological parameter but depends largely on a decision based on economic considerations. As we shall see below, dealing with the gross rather than with the net national income and investment brings this factor into focus.

It also follows from our definition of the national income that this concept includes the production of goods but not that of services, which is in line with the approach adopted in socialist countries. It is true that the production of services similar to goods, such as transportation, laundries, restaurants and even trade is included. Excluded, however, from the national income are on the one hand, government administrative services, education, entertainment, health, etc., and on the other hand, the utilization by consumers of certain fixed assets, such as dwelling-houses or hotels. All such services are, however, accounted for in the national income statistics of capitalist countries, by including in the national income government expenditure on administration, public or private expenditure on education and health, and finally private expenditure on entertainment, rents, etc.

It appears that in the study of economic dynamics the treatment of national income as production of goods offers appreciable advantages. The measurement of changes in real values – i.e. values after elimination of price changes – is generally easier for goods than for services. For instance, in the statistics of capitalist countries the real increase in administrative activity is measured by an index of employment of government officials (weighted according to their wages in the basic year) and thus no account is taken of changes in labour productivity, i.e. in the number of man-hours required for the performance of a given operation, which obviously would be fairly difficult. The same problem also emerges to some extent in the measurement of services in education, entertainment or health. From a different point of view it is inconvenient, in the analysis of economic growth, to include in the national income the services rendered by residential buildings, etc. Here, the ratio between the capital outlay and the value of services is very high in comparison to the corresponding ratio in the production of goods which, as we shall see, would considerably complicate the theory of growth. Obviously, this does not mean that services are to be neglected in long-run planning, but rather that they are planned not in terms of national income but either in terms of employment (as, e.g., administrative services) or in terms of capacity of fixed assets rendering consumer services (e.g. the services rendered by residential buildings).

2. In a closed economy the gross national income is divided, according to its final use into, the following components:

(*a*) Productive investment, i.e. outlays on reproduction and expansion of the stock of equipment (machinery and buildings) involved in the production of goods.

(*b*) Increases in inventories, i.e. the value of the increment in working capital and stocks.

(*c*) 'Non-productive' investment, i.e. outlays on new fixed assets which do not contribute to the production of goods – such as residential buildings, hotels, schools, hospitals, stadiums, streets, parks, etc.

(*d*) Collective consumption which includes non-investment goods consumed by central and local government as well as by enterprises engaged in the production of services not included in the national income. For instance, stationery used in offices, medicines, food and linen used in hospitals, stage properties in theatres, etc.

(*e*) Individual consumption of goods and similar services.

In an open economy it is necessary to add to the above (*f*) exports – i.e. the value of the output of goods which are sold abroad – and at the same time to deduct (*g*) – imports of raw materials, semi-manufactures, and finished goods, which are included in the components of the national income listed above but are not produced at home.

Thus the national income is divided as shown overleaf:

1-2

(*a*) Productive investment
(*b*) Increases in inventories
(*c*) Non-productive investment
(*d*) Collective consumption
(*e*) Individual consumption
(*f*) Exports
(*g*) Less imports
= National income

As mentioned above, both investment and national income are gross of depreciation. Some further clarification of the treatment of capital under construction is required. In the statistics of both socialist and capitalist countries changes in work in progress in machine-building are accounted for in the increase in inventories, while those in the volume of buildings under construction are included in investment. For our purpose it will be more convenient to classify the latter item under increase in inventories as well. Investment in fixed capital is thus tantamount to the volume of new capital equipment delivered in a given year.

Among the components of the national income two broad classes may be distinguished: (i) those elements which serve as the *means* to increase the national income – i.e. productive investment and increases in inventories; (ii) those which are the *aim* of production of goods – i.e. non-productive investment and collective and individual consumption. We shall call the sum of productive investment and increases in inventories *productive accumulation*, and the sum of non-productive investment and consumption – *consumption* in the broad sense.

It remains debatable, to which class – that of means or that of aims – one should assign the difference between exports and imports, i.e. the balance of trade. Since it will be assumed below that the balance of trade is equal to zero, we shall not labour this point.

3. In order to compute the national income and its components as defined above, it must be specified at what prices the goods composing the national income should be valued. In the socialist economy two distinct sets of prices are used: factory prices and market prices. Factory prices are established at the level of average costs of production *plus* a small mark-up; market

prices comprise, over and above this level, the turnover tax. Since, in practice, the turnover tax is levied mainly on consumer goods, the valuation of the national income at market prices leads to some distortions in its dynamics.

Let us suppose, for example, that a given number of workers, using a given machine, shifts from the production of investment goods to that of consumer goods. If market prices are used in the evaluation of national income, then the productivity of labour and machinery will show a spurious increase. Therefore, in studying the theory of economic growth, it is advisable to assume that national income and its components are computed at factory prices.

The next problem is the evaluation of the national income in consecutive years so as to calculate its 'real' growth, which is of interest in the study of economic dynamics. This may be achieved by valuing the national income and its components at constant prices, for instance at prices in the initial year. The method involves a certain difficulty with regard to the emergence of new products for which no prices existed in the base year. This difficulty may be dealt with by means of the following approximation. Suppose that the factory price of a new product A is, say, 10 per cent higher than that of a similar product B which existed in the initial year. We may assume that the 'base' price of A was equal to the 'base' price of B plus 10 per cent. Such a method, however, may be difficult to apply to a period rather distant from the initial year, since it may not be easy to find in the initial year any product which would be close to A. Again, however, there is a way out. The new product in the year n is defined as one that did not exist in the year $n-1$; now, in the production of year $n-1$ we can find a product B which is close to it; this product B might itself have been a new product in some previous year, but its 'base' price has already been determined by means of our method. It is easy to see that if we start from the initial year and then move onwards from year to year, we shall find no difficulty in valuing the national income and its constituents at constant prices.

5

In addition to these general problems of valuation of the national income there are two more specific ones. One concerns the increase in inventories; the other, exports and imports. As regards the former it should be kept in mind that the value of inventories at the beginning and at the end of each year is to be computed in the prices of the initial year, and only after doing this may the difference between the two be calculated.

The price problems concerning exports and imports are more complicated. First we compute the value of exports in the initial year at factory prices. The ratio of this value to the foreign exchange value of exports yields the so-called 'achieved rate of exchange'. The product of this rate and of the foreign exchange value of imports yields in turn what may be called the 'value of imports at factory prices': it is the value of such exports expressed in factory prices which would buy a given volume of imports in the initial year. It should be noted that the relation between the values of exports and imports at factory prices in that year is the same as that between their respective values in foreign currency.

How should we value exports and imports of any year at the factory prices of the initial year? At first glance the following approach appears to be reasonable. Since foreign exchange prices generally change both for exports and for imports, the value of exports is calculated at the export prices of the initial year, and the value of imports at the import prices of this year – i.e. as the 'real' values of exports and imports expressed in foreign exchange. These values are then multiplied by the 'achieved exchange rate' of the initial year and thus we obtain the values of exports and imports at the factory prices of that year.

This approach, however, has an important deficiency. If there occurs a change in the terms of trade, the ratio of export and import volumes arrived at by the above method would be different from the ratio of their actual foreign exchange values. In particular, these volumes would generally not be equal in the case of balanced foreign trade. Suppose, say, that in a given year both exports and imports amount to 1.5 billion dollars; that the index of export prices based on the initial year is 105, while that of import prices is 125; and that the 'achieved rate of exchange' for the initial year is 30 zlotys per dollar. 'Real' exports then amount to 1.5/1.05 = 1.43 billion dollars, and 'real' imports to 1.5/1.25 = 1.2 billion dollars, while their respective values at factory prices of the initial year are 43 and 36 billion zlotys.

This discrepancy can be corrected as follows: the foreign currency 'real' value of imports is calculated in constant import prices of the initial year, but the 'real' value of exports in foreign currency is assumed to bear the same relation to 'real' imports as does the current foreign currency value of exports to that of imports. If this method is used in the preceding example, 'real' exports equal 'real' imports – i.e. 1.2 billion dollars. This method may be defined as deflating exports by the index of import prices rather than by that of export prices. In our example the export value – 1.5 billion dollars – is divided by 1.25 rather than by 1.05. Thus it is clear that if exports and imports are equal in current prices their 'real values' determined in this way will also be equal.

If the current exchange value of exports amounts to, say, 0.9 of that of imports (e.g. exports are equal to 1.35 billion dollars and imports to 1.5 billion dollars) the 'real' value of exports is determined as 0.9 of the 'real' value of imports. (If the index of import prices is 1.25, 'real' exports equal 0.9 × 1.2 = 1.08, or, what amounts to the same thing, 1.35/1.25 = 1.08 billion dollars.) The 'real' value of exports thus defined indicates the value of imports at the base year's import prices which can be obtained in exchange for these exports. It is thus the so-called 'volume of the import-equivalent exports'. Finally, by multiplying the 'real' values of exports and imports by the 'achieved exchange rate' of the initial year we arrive again at the respective values at factory prices of that year.

It is obvious that the 'real' values of exports and imports – which are components of the 'real' national income – are, by definition, proportional to their respective current values in foreign currency. Thus the equilibrium in the balance of trade will have its counterpart in the equality of the respective items in the 'real' national income accounts. Any difference between these items shows the amount of foreign lending or borrowing (more precisely, such difference is equal to the volume of the import equivalent of foreign credits multiplied by the 'achieved exchange rate' of the initial year). The advantages of this approach are obtained, however, at the expense of introducing a certain modification into the concept of national income: the volume of exports ceases to be what it was in the previous approach, i.e. a measure of export output; it becomes instead a measure of the volume of imports which this output can buy. Hence, if the volume of the national output remains unchanged, but there is a deterioration in the terms of trade, the national income decreases. Thus the national income no longer represents what is produced but what is received. This is not, however, a disadvantage at all from the point of view of the study of economic growth, as we shall see below. It appears that whenever in such an analysis we deal with the problem of foreign trade, it is convenient to have changes in the terms of trade reflected in changes in the national income.

It should be added that all the imported goods which enter into different components of the national income must be valued at the same prices at which they are priced when entering into the item 'imports'. This is because the sole purpose of the deduction of the latter item from the sum total of all other components of the national income is to eliminate from them all such elements which are not produced at home. This is not achieved if these elements are not priced at strictly the same prices.

4. Henceforward in our argument we shall assume that the country considered neither borrows from nor lends to other countries so that its foreign trade is balanced. From the above definitions it follows that in such a case exports and imports as items of the 'real' national income accounts are equal. Hence, national income will be the sum of productive accumulation and consumption in the broad sense. This definitely does not

mean that in our argument we shall completely disregard the problems of foreign trade. On the contrary, as we shall see below, the necessity of balancing foreign trade plays an important part in our analysis of the determination of the rate of growth of national income.

5. The factory prices of the initial period at which, according to the above, the national income is evaluated are, broadly speaking, proportionate to the labour costs of the respective products. (Labour costs are assumed here to cover the labour required to produce materials used in the production of the goods considered.) It follows that the labour outlay per unit of national income is approximately equal for productive accumulation and for consumption in the broad sense in the initial period.†

Since in subsequent years the national income is expressed in factory prices of the initial period, the labour content per unit of national income in the two sectors will remain approximately equal only if labour productivity in these sectors increases *pari passu* so that the labour outlay per unit of national income in these sectors declines in the same proportion. (From the above argument on the subject of import prices there follows an additional condition for the approximate equality of the labour outlay per unit of national income for productive accumulation and for consumption: the foreign exchange prices of imported goods for the two sectors must bear a stable relation to one another.)

It will be assumed below that these conditions are fulfilled in the process of growth with the result that the labour outlay per unit of national income in the sectors of productive accumulation and consumption remains approximately equal. Thus to any change in the relative shares of these items in the national income there corresponds a proportionate change in the distribution of employment between the respective sectors of the economy. This has an important bearing upon our subsequent discussion.

† Because of the difference in average wages this will be true only if we measure the labour outlay not in working hours but as an equivalent in terms of simple labour, i.e. by the ratio of the wage bill to the hourly wage for unskilled labour.

9

2. BASIC EQUATIONS

1. As mentioned above, the components of productive accumulation – i.e. productive investment and increase in inventories –are a prerequisite for the growth of the national income. We shall now determine the relationship between the increase in national income and these items.

Let us denote the national income in a given year by Y; productive investment by I; the increase in inventories – i.e. working capital and stocks – by S; and consumption in the broad sense by C. According to the above definitions and assumptions we have

$$Y = I + S + C \tag{1}$$

where $I + S$ is productive accumulation.

Let us now establish the relationship between the increment in national income on the one hand, and productive investment, and the level of national income on the other. We shall denote the increment in the national income from the beginning of a given year to the beginning of the next by ΔY. Let us assume that in the course of the year the national income remains constant so that the change occurs at the beginning of the following year. Thus ΔY is also the difference between the total national income of the given year and that of the following year. This increment is due, first of all, to the productive effect of investment, I, representing the volume of equipment delivered in the course of the first year; according to our assumption this yields production starting from the beginning of the following year. Let us denote by m the so-called capital–output ratio, i.e. the capital outlay per unit increment in national income. The productive effect of investment – i.e. the amount by which the national income is increased as a result of investment – is thus $(1/m)I$.

There are, however, other factors which affect the increment in the national income. First, capital equipment is subject to continuous obsolescence and wear and tear, which results in scrapping of obsolete equipment, and thus a contraction in productive capacity.† Owing to this factor, the national income declines at the beginning of the second year by an amount aY, a being a coefficient which will be called the 'parameter of depreciation'. This process has an opposite effect from the increase in national income resulting from productive investment.

There is also a tendency for the national income to increase owing to improvements in the utilization of equipment which do not require significant capital outlays. Greater output may be obtained from existing plant due to improvements in the organization of labour, more economical use of raw materials, elimination of faulty products, etc. As a result of such efforts the national income increases at the beginning of the next year by an amount uY, u being the coefficient which represents the effect of such improvements.‡

Thus we arrive at the following formula representing the increment in the national income ΔY as a function of investment I and the level of the national income Y in a given year:

$$\Delta Y = \frac{1}{m} I - aY + uY \tag{2}$$

Let us divide both sides of equation (2) by Y:

$$\frac{\Delta Y}{Y} = \frac{1}{m} \frac{I}{Y} - a + u$$

† That part of wear and tear that is covered by current repairs (including spare parts) is deducted from the value of production, analogously to raw material inputs, in order to arrive at gross national income. Thus we are considering here only that part of wear and tear that occurs *despite* current repairs.

‡ The coefficient u reflects *inter alia* progress made in avoiding bottlenecks, which hamper the full utilization of productive capacity. If, for example, the productive capacity for good A is not dovetailed with that for good B, so that output of B lags behind that of A, this will inhibit the full utilization of the productive capacity for A. Such disproportions should not arise in a perfectly planned economy, but in practice differences in the fulfilment of plans for the production of particular commodities, imperfect foresight of developments in overseas markets, etc. make bottlenecks unavoidable. Progress in reducing these discrepancies will lead to a gradual improvement in the utilization of total capital equipment, and will thus account for part of u.

If we denote by r the rate of growth of the national income we obtain

$$r = \frac{1}{m}\frac{I}{Y} - a + u \tag{3}$$

2. At this point the question arises whether formula (3) may also be used for the analysis of the dynamics of a capitalist economy. The answer is in the negative; the difference between the capitalist and the socialist system will make its appearance in the interpretation given to the coefficient u.

In the socialist system the productive capacity is, at least in principle, fully utilized. Nevertheless owing to improvements in the organization of labour, to more economical use of raw materials, etc., a steady increase may be achieved in the national income through better use of existing equipment. If such progress goes on at a uniform rate, u remains constant.

By contrast, in the capitalist system the degree of utilization of equipment depends first and foremost on the relation between effective demand and the volume of productive capacity. Thus u is not an independent coefficient in this case but reflects changes in the degree to which it is possible to find a market for the output of the existing productive facilities. It is only in the socialist economy, where utilization of productive capacity is safe-guarded by the plan (first and foremost by fixing an appropriate relation between prices and wages) that the coefficient u begins to reflect solely the effect of organizational and technical improvements which do not require significant capital outlays.

3. On the assumption of constant m, a and u it follows directly from formula (3), that, if the relative share of investment in the national income I/Y remains unaltered, the rate of growth r does not change either. But the constancy of I/Y is tantamount to investment growing *pari passu* with the national income.

Thus if investment is increased at the same rate as the national income, a constant rate of growth of the latter is warranted. If, however, the former expands more rapidly than the latter so that its relative share in the national income is increasing, then according to formula (3), this permits the rate of growth of national income to rise steadily – i.e. it sustains accelerating growth.

All this is valid as long as the parameters *m*, *a* and *u* remain unchanged. But is not the assumption of a constant capital–output ratio *m* in conflict with the very essence of technical progress which involves rising productivity of labour, accompanied by an increase in capital per worker?

However, the constancy of *m* merely means that the ratio of capital to output remains unchanged, which by no means excludes the possibility of a decrease in employment in relation both to output and to capital. In such a case employment would fall in the same proportion with respect both to capital and output, so that labour productivity would increase *pari passu* with the capital–labour ratio. Indeed, historical and statistical evidence, both from capitalist and socialist countries, shows that there is no need for the capital–output ratio *m* to increase in order to sustain a steady rise in labour productivity. These remarks on technical progress are merely introductory, and the problem will be treated in more detail in Chapter 7.

4. We shall now briefly consider the relationship between increments in national income and the other component of productive accumulation, i.e. the increase in inventories. We may assume that the volume of inventories, given the physical structure, rises proportionally to the national income, so that the increase in inventories, *S*, is proportional to the increment in the national income:

$$S = \mu \Delta Y \tag{4}$$

where μ is the ratio between the volume of inventories and the national income – i.e. the so-called 'average period of turnover' of inventories.

The period of turnover of inventories will be different for different goods, from which it follows that the coefficient μ depends upon the physical structure of the increase in inventories. In what follows we shall disregard the effect of changes in this structure upon the parameter μ. It should, however, be noted that this is a rather far-reaching simplification – the more so if it is recalled that inventories are meant to include the volume of capital under construction. The ratio between this volume and current outlays on construction being relatively high, shifts from consumption to investment in the composition of national income – with which we shall deal frequently in our discussion – must lead to an increase in μ. In accordance with the assumption made above, however, for the sake of simplicity we shall not take this into account.

It should be noted that a similar simplifying assumption is made with regard to the capital–output ratio, m, which also depends on the structure of investment. It is true that the co-efficient m, in contrast to μ, does not necessarily increase when there is a shift from consumption to investment in the composition of national income, since the production of finished investment goods, such as machinery and buildings – integrated over all stages of production – is hardly more capital intensive than that of consumer goods. (On the other hand, the capital–output ratio is generally higher in primary products than in higher stages of production.) In any case, in our analysis we disregard the effects of changes in the structure of investment on the capital–output ratio m.

5. Starting with equations (3) and (4) we may now establish the relationship between the rate of growth of national income and the relative share of productive accumulation in the national income. Equation (3) may be rewritten as follows:

$$\frac{I}{Y} = (r + a - u)\,m$$

and equation (4) in the form

$$\frac{S}{Y} = \frac{\mu \Delta Y}{Y} = \mu r$$

By adding these equations we obtain

$$\frac{I+S}{Y} = (m + \mu)\,r + (a - u)\,m$$

and thus
$$r = \frac{1}{m+\mu} \cdot \frac{I+S}{Y} - \frac{m}{m+\mu}\,(a - u) \qquad (5)$$

$I+S$ is productive accumulation, and we denote by i its relative share in the national income, i.e.

$$i = \frac{I+S}{Y}$$

Since the national income Y is the sum of productive accumulation, $I+S$, and consumption in the broad sense, C, the relative share of consumption in national income will be

$$\frac{C}{Y} = 1 - i \tag{6}$$

For the sake of brevity, we shall call the relative share of productive accumulation in the national income the 'rate of productive accumulation'. Let us, moreover, denote $m+\mu$ by k; we shall call k the 'capital–output ratio for total capital', since it indicates the amount of fixed capital and inventories required to produce a unit increment in the national income. By introducing these symbols in equation (5) we obtain

$$r = \frac{i}{k} - \frac{m}{k}(a-u) \tag{7}$$

It will be seen from this equation that, if the parameters k, m, a and u remain constant, in order to sustain a constant rate of growth the relative share of productive accumulation in the national income must be kept at a constant level. This means that, in the case of a constant rate of growth, productive accumulation increases *pari passu* with the national income – i.e. at a rate r.

It has been demonstrated above that in such a case productive investment increases in step with the national income; thus the same must be true of the other component of productive accumulation – i.e. the increase in inventories. Moreover, since the relative share of consumption in the national income, $1-i$, also stays constant, it is clear that consumption also rises *pari passu* with the national income.

If, however, the growth in the national income is accelerated, i.e. the rate r is rising, the relative share of productive accumulation in national income i must also rise. Thus, in this case, productive accumulation rises more rapidly than the national income, while consumption grows more slowly, its share in the national income, $1 - i$, showing a steady decline.

The higher the constant rate of growth of national income r, the greater must be the share of productive accumulation i in national income, and the lower the relative share of consumption $1 - i$. This fact alone points to certain limitations in the choice of a rate of growth. If this rate is raised the relative share of consumption in the national income must be reduced, which adversely affects the level of consumption in the short run. This is one of the factors which must be taken into account when making a decision on the rate of growth. The determination of the rate of growth (which also depends upon the balance of manpower and the balance of trade) is the main topic of this book, but, before concentrating upon it, it is useful to examine more closely the process of economic growth characterized by a *given*, constant rate of growth r.

3. UNIFORM GROWTH

1. We shall now consider the process of economic growth given the following assumptions:

    (*a*) The rate of growth, *r*, of the national income is constant.

    (*b*) The parameters m, k, a and u remain unaltered.

    (*c*) The productivity of labour in new plant which is brought into operation in successive years increases at a constant rate α owing to technical progress (inclusive of organizational progress). In other words, the productivity of labour in the establishments brought into operation in a given year is $(1+\alpha)$ times higher than that in the establishments brought into operation in the preceding year. (In accordance with the assumptions made at the end of Chapter 1 we postulate that the rate of the increase in productivity of labour is the same for the sector of productive accumulation and that of consumption in the broad sense.)

It follows from assumptions (*a*) and (*b*) that productive accumulation and its components – productive investment and increase in inventories – as well as consumption rise at a constant rate *r*. We shall now prove that the same is true of the stock of fixed capital K, provided that its life-span, *n*, remains unchanged.†

The stock of fixed capital existing at a given time consists of investment carried out in the course of the preceding *n* years, since all plant constructed earlier has already gone out of use. Let us denote by K_t the stock of fixed capital at the time *t*; by I_1 investment in the first year of the *n*-year period preceding the moment *t*; by I_2 investment in the second year of this period and so on. Thus we have

$$K_t = I_1 + I_2 + I_3 + \ldots + I_n$$

† As we shall see *ex post*, the constancy of this life-span is inherent in the constancy of the rate of growth *r* and the parameters *a* and *u*. If *n* varied with constant *r* and *u*, the parameter of depreciation *a* would also vary.

Since investment increases at the annual rate r, we obtain

$$K_t = I_1[1 + (1+r) + (1+r)^2 + \ldots + (1+r)^{n-1}] \qquad (8)$$

Shifting the sequence of investment by one year, we obtain for time $t+1$

$$K_{t+1} = I_2 + I_3 + I_4 + \ldots + I_{n+1}$$
$$= I_2[1 + (1+r) + (1+r)^2 + \ldots + (1+r)^{n-1}]$$

Dividing this equation by the preceding one we arrive at

$$\frac{K_{t+1}}{K_t} = \frac{I_2}{I_1}$$

Since I_2 is the investment made a year later than I_1, and investment increases at the annual rate r it follows that

$$\frac{K_{t+1}}{K_t} = 1 + r \qquad (9)$$

Thus the stock of fixed capital also increases at a rate r.

It is of interest now to find the relationship between the national income and the stock of fixed capital. Our discussion of this relationship will serve also to prepare the ground for the solution of our next problem: that of the rate of growth of average labour productivity for the economy (our assumption on the uniform growth of the productivity of labour pertains only to productivity in the new establishments brought into operation in successive years).

2. Let us consider the output which corresponds to each of the components of the stock of fixed capital K_t, i.e. to $I_1, I_2, \ldots, I_n$ in the year $t+1$. The equipment represented by these investment outlays yielded – according to our definition in section 1 of Chapter 2 – at the beginning of the next year the output

$$\frac{1}{m}I_1, \qquad \frac{1}{m}I_2, \qquad \ldots, \qquad \frac{1}{m}I_n$$

respectively (where m is the capital–output ratio). With the lapse of time, however, owing to improvements in the utilization of equipment, the respective outputs were increasing every year at a rate u during the subsequent lifetime of the plant. Now, the equipment represented by investment in the first year of the n-year period which preceded the moment t, i.e. by I_1, was kept in operation up to the time $t+1$, i.e. for n years. Similarly, equipment represented by investment of the next year, i.e. by I_2, was kept in operation for $n-1$ years; that of the third year for $n-2$ years; and so on. Consequently, in the year $t+1$ the output of the plant represented by investment I_1 will be

$$\frac{1}{m} I_1(1+u)^{n-1},$$

that of I_2 will be
$$\frac{1}{m} I_2(1+u)^{n-2},$$

etc. Hence, aggregate output or national income, in the year $t+1$ amounts to

$$Y_{t+1} = \frac{1}{m} I_1(1+u)^{n-1} + \frac{1}{m} I_2(1+u)^{n-2} + \dots + \frac{1}{m} I_n$$

Taking into consideration that investment increases at an annual rate r, we obtain for the national income†

$$Y_{t+1} = \frac{1}{m} I_1[(1+u)^{n-1} + (1+r)(1+u)^{n-2}$$
$$+ (1+r)^2(1+u)^{n-3} + \dots + (1+r)^{n-1}] \quad (10)$$

† This formula may serve to obtain an expression for the parameter a as a function of n, r and u. As defined above, a is the ratio of the decrement of national income, which results from discarding old equipment, to the national income. This decrement is equal to the output of the oldest generation of plant, i.e.

$$\frac{1}{m} I_1(1+u)^{n-1}.$$

Dividing this expression by the value of the national income as given by formula (10) we obtain

$$a = \frac{\frac{1}{m} I_1(1+u)^{n-1}}{\frac{1}{m} I_1[(1+u)^{n-1} + (1+r)(1+u)^{n-2} + \dots + (1+r)^{n-1}]}$$
$$= \frac{1}{1 + \frac{1+r}{1+u} + \left(\frac{1+r}{1+u}\right)^2 + \dots + \left(\frac{1+r}{1+u}\right)^{n-1}}$$

Dividing equation (10) by equation (8) we obtain the ratio between the national income in the year $t+1$ and the stock of fixed capital at time t:

$$\frac{Y_{t+1}}{K_t} = \frac{1}{m} \frac{(1+u)^{n-1} + (1+r)(1+u)^{n-2} + \ldots + (1+r)^{n-1}}{1 + (1+r) + \ldots + (1+r)^{n-1}}$$

(11)

It is immediately obvious that this ratio does not depend upon t, in other words it remains constant. This was to be expected, since we made the assumption that the national income grew at an annual rate r and we proved that the same was true for the stock of fixed capital. It will be noticed, moreover, that each term in the numerator of the fraction by which $1/m$ is multiplied, is greater than the corresponding term of the denominator (e.g. $(1+u)^{n-1} > 1$, etc.). Thus the numerator is greater than the denominator and, consequently, the ratio of the national income to the stock of fixed capital is greater than the reciprocal of the capital–output ratio

$$\frac{Y_{t+1}}{K_t} > \frac{1}{m}$$

This obviously results from the improvement in the utilization of the old equipment at an annual rate u. If u equals zero, it follows from formula (11) that

$$\frac{Y_{t+1}}{K_t} = \frac{1}{m} \dagger$$

and, after having summed the geometrical progression in the denominator,

$$a = \frac{r-u}{\left[\left(\frac{1+r}{1+u}\right)^n - 1\right](1+u)}$$

As will be seen from this formula, n is fully determined by a, r and u. Hence from the assumption that the latter are constant it follows that the life-span of equipment also remains unaltered (cf. note 1 on p. 17).

† It may seem strange that greater output per unit of investment is produced from old machinery than from new. First of all, it is quite possible that the production process has been more fully mastered with older equipment. This, however, is only a minor factor in explaining the 'paradox'; in reality many of the improvements in the utilization of equipment and organization of labour are also adopted

3. Let us now consider the problem of the increase in the average productivity of labour for the economy as a whole. It was assumed above that labour productivity in plants brought into operation in successive years increases at a constant rate – i.e. that in any given year it is higher than it was a year before in the proportion $(1 + \alpha)$. Now, the output produced by new plant in any given year is $(1 + r)$ times greater than that which came out of new plant in the preceding year, since investment increases at an annual rate r and the capital–output ratio m is constant. But, if both output and labour productivity increase at constant rates in the new plants brought into operation each year, the same must be true of employment. Indeed, if we denote the rate of increase in employment in new plant by ϵ we may write

$$1 + \epsilon = \frac{1 + r}{1 + \alpha} \qquad (12)$$

Fixed capital at the time t consists, as we explained above, of equipment represented by investment $I_1, I_2, \ldots, I_n$. Let us denote by $z_1, z_2, \ldots, z_n$ the corresponding levels of employment immediately after the new equipment is brought into operation. It follows from the above that these levels of employment represent a geometrical progression with a ratio $1 + \epsilon$. Let us for a moment make an assumption which will substantially simplify the argument. According to the above, output from existing plant increases at an annual rate u, e.g. owing to improvements in the organization of labour. Let us assume that the productivity of labour in existing plants rises at the same rate u, so that employment remains unchanged from the time they were brought into operation. In this special case, the levels of employment which correspond to the equipment represented by investment $I_1, I_2, \ldots, I_n$, are at time t the same as at the time when the respective plants were brought into operation – i.e. they remain

with new equipment. The constancy of m means that if this factor were not taken into account in the capital–output ratio, it would have to increase over time. This also explains another 'paradox': that the ratio of the national income to aggregate fixed capital remains unaltered despite a steady improvement in the utilization of equipment.

equal to $z_1, z_2, ..., z_n$. Hence, total employment at the time t (denoted by Z_t) is

$$Z_t = z_1 + z_2 + z_3 + ... + z_n$$

But since $z_1, z_2, ..., z_n$ represent a geometrical progression with a ratio $1 + \epsilon$ we have

$$Z_t = z_1[1 + (1 + \epsilon) + (1 + \epsilon)^2 + ... + (1 + \epsilon)^{n-1}] \qquad (13)$$

Similarly, for the time $t + 1$ we obtain

$$Z_{t+1} = z_2[1 + (1 + \epsilon) + (1 + \epsilon)^2 + ... + (1 + \epsilon)^{n-1}]$$

and, dividing the latter equation by the former,

$$\frac{Z_{t+1}}{Z_t} = \frac{z_2}{z_1}$$

But since z_2 represents employment in establishments brought into operation a year later than those represented by z_1 we have

$$\frac{Z_{t+1}}{Z_t} = 1 + \epsilon \qquad (14)$$

Thus, aggregate employment increases at a rate ϵ, i.e. *pari passu* with employment in the new establishments brought into operation. This is exactly analogous to the relation between the stock of fixed capital and investment, which both increase at a rate r.

Moreover, since the national income increases annually in the proportion $1 + r$ and total employment in the proportion $1 + \epsilon$, overall labour productivity increases annually in the proportion $(1 + r)/(1 + \epsilon)$ and thus according to equation (12) in the proportion $1 + \alpha$, i.e. *pari passu* with labour productivity in new plants as they are brought successively into operation. It should be recalled that this is valid only in the case of uniform growth considered in this chapter. However, as we shall prove below, this result does not depend on our temporary assumption that labour productivity in existing plants increases at the same rate u as the output of these plants.

4. In fact the productivity of labour working with old equipment does not necessarily increase at a rate u. If, for

example, the run of machines is accelerated, this does not necessarily mean that productivity of labour is increased in the same proportion, as it may prove necessary to hire additional workers. On the other hand, increased intensity of labour may not lead to an increase in output but to a reduction of employment; this is the case where, for example, an increased number of looms is run by each worker. In the general case, therefore, labour productivity in old establishments will be rising at a rate w different from u.† As a result, employment in the old establishments does not remain stable, but changes in the proportion $(1+u)/(1+w)$ p.a. It follows that employment levels on machinery of different ages at the time t are not $z_1, z_2, ..., z_n$ but

$$z_1 \left(\frac{1+u}{1+w}\right)^{n-1}, \quad z_2 \left(\frac{1+u}{1+w}\right)^{n-2}, \quad ..., \quad z_n$$

while aggregate employment Z_t is

$$Z_t = z_1 \left(\frac{1+u}{1+w}\right)^{n-1} + z_2 \left(\frac{1+u}{1+w}\right)^{n-2} + ... + z_n$$

Finally, taking into acount that $z_1, z_2, ..., z_n$ form a geometrical progression with a ratio $1+\epsilon$ we obtain

$$Z_t = z_1 \left[\left(\frac{1+u}{1+w}\right)^{n-1} + (1+\epsilon)\left(\frac{1+u}{1+w}\right)^{n-2} + ... + (1+\epsilon)^{n-1}\right]$$

$$(15)$$

(The formula we arrived at is analogous to formula (10) for the national income.) Similarly, for time $t+1$ we obtain

$$Z_{t+1} = z_2 \left[\left(\frac{1+u}{1+w}\right)^{n-1} + (1+\epsilon)\left(\frac{1+u}{1+w}\right)^{n-2} + ... + (1+\epsilon)^{n-1}\right]$$

and, dividing this equation by the former,

$$\frac{Z_{t+1}}{Z_t} = \frac{z_2}{z_1} = 1+\epsilon \qquad (14')$$

Thus we have obtained the same result as in the special case

† If $w > u$, this augments the supply of labour for employment in new plant; if $w < u$, the reverse is the case.

previously considered; again, the overall productivity of labour increases from year to year in the proportion

$$\frac{1+r}{1+\epsilon} = 1+\alpha \tag{12'}$$

Hence, total employment and the overall productivity of labour increase *pari passu* with employment and labour productivity in new plant.

5. According to our assumptions of uniform growth, the rate of growth of the national income r, and the parameters m, k, u and a, as well as the rate of increase of labour productivity in the new plants brought into operation, α, are constant. We have also proved that the overall labour productivity increases at a rate α. We shall now make the additional assumption that full employment prevails in the economy. We shall write β for the rate of growth of manpower.

The rate of increase in employment denoted above by ϵ concerns in fact merely the employment in the production of goods. We shall assume, however, that employment in services increases *pari passu* – i.e. at a rate ϵ. For full employment to be maintained, the rate of growth of employment must be equal to that of manpower, and so we have

$$\epsilon = \beta \tag{16}$$

and

$$1+r = (1+\alpha)(1+\beta) = 1+\alpha+\beta+\alpha\beta \tag{17}$$

Since we postulated the constancy of the two rates of growth – that of national income, r, and that of labour productivity, α – as a characteristic of uniform growth, under full employment we must also postulate the constancy of β. The annual rates of growth α and β being rather small fractions, we may disregard their product $\alpha\beta$ in equation (17), and write the latter in an approximate form

$$r = \alpha+\beta \tag{17'}$$

Thus, the rate of growth of national income r is determined jointly by α which depends upon technical progress and β (which depends upon the natural rate of growth of the labour

Uniform growth

force). On the other hand, given the parameters m, k, u and a, the rate of growth r determines the constant share of productive accumulation, i, in the national income, which is necessary in order to sustain it, on the basis of the equation

$$r = \frac{1}{k}i - \frac{m}{k}(a-u) \qquad (7)$$

This determination of i is represented graphically in Fig. 1 where i is plotted as the abscissa, and r as the ordinate.

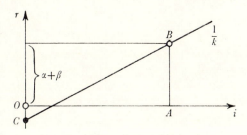

Fig. 1

The straight line representing the linear function given by formula (7) has the slope $1/k$ and intersects the r-axis at a point C situated at a distance $m/k(a-u)$ below the origin.† The rate of productive accumulation which corresponds to the rate of growth $r = a + \beta$ is $i = OA$.

As long as our two conditions – that of constancy of the parameters m, k, a and u, and that of full employment – are fulfilled, acceleration of growth over and above the rate r is impossible, since it would come up against the barrier of a manpower shortage. There would, therefore, be no sense in raising the relative share of productive accumulation in the national income in order to accelerate the rate of growth. In these circumstances it would lead only to the creation of idle productive capacity.

It is obvious that when we remove our rigid assumptions as to the constancy of parameters and full employment, the problem

† This is the case when $a - u > 0$. If $a - u < 0$ the point C is, of course, situated above the origin o.

of the choice of a rate of growth will emerge. We shall deal with this in the chapters that follow. We shall begin by examining the situation where there is a reserve of labour. We shall then proceed to discuss the case where no such reserve exists, and where in order to accelerate the rate of growth, it is necessary to overcome the shortage of labour – for example by raising the capital–output ratio.

4. INCREASING THE RATE OF GROWTH OF NATIONAL INCOME UNDER CONDITIONS OF AN UNLIMITED SUPPLY OF LABOUR

1. With constant parameters m, k, a and u, and under conditions of full employment, the rate of growth of national income cannot, as was shown above, exceed the level $\alpha + \beta$, where α stands for the rate of increase of productivity and β for that of the labour force. Any higher rate would prove impossible because of the emergence of a shortage of labour. We shall now consider a situation characterized by the existence of a reserve of manpower – e.g. married women who would be willing to take up jobs if these were easily accessible, some surplus of labour in agriculture, etc. By drawing on such reserves it is possible to raise the rate of growth of employment above β, and thus raise the rate of growth of the national income r above $\alpha + \beta$. It is obvious that this merely shifts the barrier of the supply of labour through time; when the reserve is exhausted we go back to the situation in which the rate of growth is $r_0 = \alpha + \beta$. However, the consequence of the higher rate of growth during the period over which the labour reserve is being absorbed will be to achieve an additional increase in the level of the national income.

2. In order to simplify the problem we shall initially ignore the possibility of exhausting the labour reserve – i.e. we assume that the reserve is so large that it cannot be exhausted even within a very long period of time. We thus disregard temporarily all problems related to the barrier of labour shortage, which enables us to concentrate upon other factors limiting the rate of growth.

Such a basic factor is that in order to raise the rate of growth r it is necessary – according to equation (7) – to increase the rate of

A socialist economy

productive accumulation i (i.e. the relative share of productive accumulation in the national income). Let us denote by i_0 the rate of productive accumulation which corresponds to the rate of growth of national income $r_0 = \alpha + \beta$. If, by raising the rate of growth of employment, we increase the rate of growth of the national income to the level $r = OL$, then i must be raised from OA to OM (see Fig. 2).†

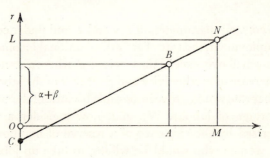

FIG. 2

But the rise in the relative share of productive accumulation in the national income means, of course, an equal decline in the relative

† This is a slightly oversimplified presentation of the problem of raising the rate of growth of the national income. In order to increase r to the level OL, the rate of productive accumulation i is initially increased, as mentioned in the text, to the level OM. It is, however, apparent that as a result of the more rapid increase in the national income, while the life-span of equipment remains unaltered at n, the straight line CN will be shifting upwards (keeping the same slope), because the depreciation parameter a in the equation

$$r = \frac{1}{k}i - \frac{m}{k}(a-u)$$

will be declining. Indeed, a could only remain constant if the rate of growth also remained constant at r_0; the increase in the rate of growth to the level OL means that the scrapping of old productive capacity which corresponds to the life-span u will be associated with a higher level of national income than would have been the case had the rate of growth been maintained at the level r_0. Thus CN shifts upwards, and the rate of accumulation i is somewhat lower than OM. This situation will continue for n years, at the end of which time all the equipment constructed before the raising of the rate of growth will have been scrapped. The rate of accumulation will then return towards the level OM and, after some fluctuations, will eventually be stabilized. (Its level will, however, still be a little lower than OM, because with uniform growth a is a decreasing function of r; cf. note †, p. 19.)

share of consumption. This deterioration in the consumption situation in the short run is the price to be paid for increasing the rate of growth of the national income, and thus also the level of consumption in the long run, the latter being favourably affected by the cumulative effect of a higher rate of growth of national income. Thus the decision as to the level of r involves a compromise between the adverse short-run and favourable long-run effect of the higher rate of growth. Before embarking upon the analysis of the process of making this decision we must analyse more precisely the effects of a higher or lower rate of growth upon consumption.

3. Let us suppose that the national income grows at a constant rate r. At time t it will therefore equal $Y_0(1+r)^t$, where Y_0 is the initial level of income. Since the relative share of consumption in the national income is maintained at $1-i$, the level of consumption at time t will be $(1-i)Y_0(1+r)^t$. If the rate of growth is raised to r', the relative share of accumulation in the national income must correspondingly be increased to i', so that after t years the level of consumption will be $(1-i')Y_0(1+r')^t$. If we denote by C_t and C'_t the alternative levels of consumption at time t, we have the following relationships:

$$C_t = Y_0(1-i)(1+r)^t$$
$$C'_t = Y_0(1-i')(1+r')^t$$

These equations can be represented diagrammatically, for which purpose it is more convenient to work with the logarithms of consumption. We have

$$\log C_t = \log Y_0 + \log(1-i) + t\log(1+r)$$

and $$\log C'_t = \log Y_0 + \log(1-i') + t\log(1+r')$$

to which correspond in Fig. 3 the straight lines C_t and C'_t, with slopes $\log(1+r)$ and $\log(1+r')$ respectively.

It is apparent that with a higher rate of growth the level of consumption is less favourable over the period OP, i.e. the abscissa of the point of intersection Q, and more favourable thereafter;

the relative advantage is the higher, the more remote the period considered. This demonstrates the conflict between consumption in the short period and in the long period.

4. The decision concerning the rate of growth can be approached in the following way. Let us suppose that a certain rate of growth t is considered admissible, and raising the rate to $r + \Delta r$ is under examination, where Δr is a small increment. This

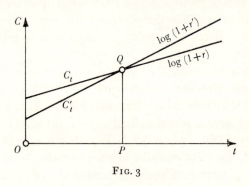

Fig. 3

would imply the necessity of increasing the rate of productive accumulation by Δi. If we denote the present level of national income by Y_0, then consumption is equal to $(1 - i)Y_0$; thus it will have to be reduced by a fraction $\Delta i/(1 - i)$. This is the loss which must be compared with the advantage of increasing the rate of growth by Δr. We may write that on balance the net advantage is

$$\Delta r - \omega \frac{\Delta i}{1 - i}.$$

where ω is a coefficient which is the higher the stronger are the objections against reducing consumption in the short run. If our problem is that of deciding how far the rate of growth is to be raised above the level $r_0 = \alpha + \beta$, we may postulate that ω will be the higher, the greater becomes the difference between i and i_0. Indeed, the further we move away from the initial situation, the more important become the objections against further reducing the relative share of consumption in the national income.

30

Thus we may rewrite the above expression as follows:

$$\Delta r - \frac{\omega(i)}{1-i}\Delta i \tag{18}$$

where $\omega(i)$ is an increasing function. If this expression is positive, it is advisable to raise i up to the point at which

$$\Delta r - \frac{\omega(i)}{1-i}\Delta i = 0$$

or

$$\frac{\Delta r}{\Delta i} = \frac{\omega(i)}{1-i} \tag{19}$$

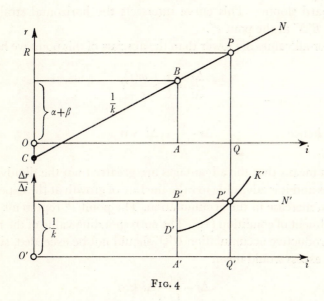

FIG. 4

This is the condition which determines the 'correct' i. The ratio $\Delta r/\Delta i$ is simply the yield in terms of an increase in the rate of growth of national income, Δr, of raising the rate of accumulation by Δi.

We shall now represent diagrammatically the process of determining the rate of accumulation and the rate of growth.

The diagram consists of two parts: the upper part is identical with Fig. 2 and in the lower part we plot i as the abscissa (as in the upper part of the diagram), whilst as the ordinate we have $\Delta r/\Delta i$. To the straight line BN, which represents the relationship between r and i in the upper part of the diagram, there corresponds a horizontal line $B'N'$ in the lower part. The distance between the latter and the i-axis is $1/k$, for this is the slope of the straight line BN. This represents the magnitude of $\Delta r/\Delta i$ as determined by equation (7). The curve $D'K'$ represents the function $\omega i/(1-i)$. Since $\omega(i)$ is assumed to be an increasing function and the denominator $1-i$ decreases when i rises, $\omega(i)/(1-i)$ is also an increasing function and the curve $D'K'$ is upward sloping. This curve intersects the horizontal straight line $B'N'$ at the pont P'.

For all values of i lower than the abscissa of this point we have

$$\frac{\Delta r}{\Delta i} = \frac{1}{k} > \frac{\omega(i)}{1-i}$$

and hence

$$\Delta r - \frac{\omega(i)}{1-i} \Delta i > 0$$

This means that the advantages are greater than the disadvantages and it is advisable to raise the rate of growth at the expense of an increase in the accumulation. The point P' represents the fulfilment of condition (19). The corresponding value of the rate of productive accumulation $O'Q'$ should not be exceeded, since any excess would mean

$$\Delta r - \frac{\omega(i)}{1-i} \Delta i < 0$$

We shall find r by projecting the point P' onto the straight line BN in the upper part of the diagram; this gives us the point P whose ordinate OR is equal to r. We shall call the curve $D'K'$ the 'government decision curve', since it shows what value of $\Delta r/\Delta i$ will satisfy the government for a given i. Hence, together with the value of $\Delta r/\Delta i$ which is determined by the conditions of production (in our case by the value of the capital–output ratio k), it forms the basis for the decision as to the rate of productive accumulation i and the rate of growth r.

5. So far, for the sake of simplicity, we have presented the process of increasing the rate of productive accumulation as an abrupt reduction of consumption from the initial position. If such were in fact the case, the decision curve would slope upwards rather steeply with the result that the rate of growth decided upon would be not much higher than $r_0 = \alpha + \beta$, for any large increase in i would lead to a prohibitive deterioration in current consumption, and consequently in real wages.

This difficulty may be avoided if the relative share of productive accumulation in the national income is raised gradually. Let us suppose that consumption increases in step with employment. It follows that the ratio of the national income to consumption increases more rapidly because of the rise in productivity of labour at a rate α p.a. At time t this ratio will have increased in the proportion $(1 + \alpha)^t$. Initially the relative share of consumption in the national income is $1 - i_0$. If the relative share of productive accumulation in the national income is raised to i, the share of consumption must, of course, decline to $1 - i$. The ratio of the national income to consumption is then to be increased from $1/(1 - i_0)$ to $1/(1 - i)$, i.e. in the proportion $(1 - i_0)/(1 - i)$. We can achieve this by raising consumption *pari passu* with employment rather than with the national income for a sufficiently long period. The length of this transition period τ is determined by the equation

$$(1 + \alpha)^\tau = \frac{1 - i_0}{1 - i}$$

or
$$\tau \log (1 + \alpha) = \log \frac{1 - i_0}{1 - i}$$

From this we obtain

$$\tau = \log \frac{1 - i_0}{1 - i} \cdot \frac{1}{\log (1 + \alpha)}$$

Since α is a small fraction, the term $\log (1 + \alpha)$ is approximately equal to α ('log' here means the natural logarithm). We thus obtain the following approximation

$$\tau = \frac{1}{\alpha}\cdot\log\frac{1-i_0}{1-i} \qquad (20)$$

which shows that τ is approximately proportionate to the reciprocal of the rate of growth of the productivity of labour.[†]

This result is of some significance for our argument. If we assume that the restraining of consumption which is necessary to increase the rate of growth is carried out in the way outlined above, the objections against raising the relative share of productive accumulation in the national income will be the stronger, the longer is the period τ during which real wages do not rise. But since the length of the period is proportional to the reciprocal of the rate of growth of productivity α, the coefficient $\omega(i)$ for a given i will be the higher, the lower is α. In other words, the lower the rate of increase in productivity of labour, the higher the ordinates of the curve $D'K'$ corresponding to given levels of the

† The acceleration of the rate of growth of productive investment which takes place in the transition period cannot immediately follow the decision to raise the rate of productive accumulation, because of the time necessary for the construction of new plant. (Let us recall that the term 'investment' is used throughout the book to mean the volume of equipment delivered in a given year; the increase in the capital under construction is included in the 'increase in inventories'; see Chapter 1, section 2.) Thus, during an interval equal to the period of construction, no acceleration of either the growth of productive investment or of the national income takes place. However, the increase in capital under construction is accelerated while that in other inventories is slowed down, the total increase in inventories remaining unaltered. Indeed, according to our assumption that the total increase in inventories is proportional to the increase in the national income irrespective of the changes in its structure, this total increase in inventories will not be accelerated during the 'preliminary' period equal to the period of construction. It follows that during this period real wages are still rising at an undiminished rate. Their increase is stopped only when the accelerated growth of investment begins to take place; from this moment on, during period τ, real wages are kept at a constant level. Thus, the period of stability in real wages is not lengthened by taking into account the period of construction, only its beginning is postponed with regard to the moment of making the decision on raising the rate of growth.

In reality a shift from consumption to investment *does* lead to an accelerated rise in the increase in inventories, since the ratio of capital under construction to investment is higher than the corresponding ratio of consumption to its inventories, which, for the sake of simplicity, we did not take into account (see Chapter 2, section 4). Hence the situation with respect to real wages during the transition towards a higher rate of growth is less favourable in reality than that resulting from our simplifying assumption.

rate of productive accumulation. As a result the lower the rate of increase in productivity α, the lower will be the level chosen for the rate of growth r as determined by the point of intersection of this curve and the straight line $B'N'$.

This should not, however, be construed as a recommendation to raise the rate of increase in productivity of labour α which is the result of technical progress with a constant capital–output ratio, and should, therefore, rather be treated as given (on this point see Chapter 7).

6. It is not out of place here to add a few observations on the nature of the 'government decision curve'. Its general features follow directly from our argument – namely that it is upward-sloping and that the lower is the rate of increase in productivity the higher are its ordinates corresponding to given levels of the rate of productive accumulation i. But is it possible to draw this curve in a precise fashion? Are its ordinates determined quantitatively similarly to those of the line CN which represents the relationship between the rate of growth r and the rate of productive accumulation i? The answer is definitely in the negative. Our curve serves only to illustrate the attitude of the government towards 'sacrificing the present for the future'. Even after the decision has been made we know only the point of intersection of the 'government decision curve' with the line $B'N'$, and the fact that at a higher rate of productive accumulation the balance of advantages and disadvantages (as expressed by formula (18)) would be negative, whilst at a lower rate it would be positive, which means that the curve is upward-sloping. In the former case its ordinate $\omega(i)/(1-i)$ is greater than $\Delta r/\Delta i = 1/k$ and thus

$$\omega(i)\frac{\Delta(i)}{1-i} > \Delta r$$

while in the latter case the reverse is true.

The main advantages of using the 'government decision curve' in our analysis will be seen in the discussion of cases where the relationship between the rate of growth r and the rate of productive accumulation i differs from that represented by the line *BN* (e.g. in the discussion of the problem of the effect of difficulties in balancing foreign trade or that of labour shortage). Indeed, the concept of the 'decision curve' will then enable us to show the effects of the changes in the relationship between r and i on the choice of the rate of growth of national income, given the attitude of the government towards 'sacrificing the present for the future'.

5. INCREASING THE RATE OF GROWTH OF NATIONAL INCOME UNDER CONDITIONS OF A LIMITED RESERVE OF LABOUR

1. In the preceding chapter we assumed that there existed an unlimited supply of labour. We shall now consider the more realistic case of a limited reserve of labour. Thus if the rate of growth r exceeds the level $r_0 = \alpha + \beta$ this reserve will eventually be exhausted. The rate of growth of national income then returns, as described above, to the level r_0. Simultaneously the relative share of productive accumulation in the national income falls back to i_0, and the relative share of consumption to $1 - i_0$. The result of this process is that there is an additional increase in the national income to the extent corresponding to the excess of labour force over actual employment in the initial position. Since after the exhaustion of the reserve the relative share of consumption in the national income regains the level $1 - i_0$, it follows that the additional proportional increase in consumption (as compared with growth at a rate r_0) is the same as that of the national income.

We may illustrate this by the following example in which the discussion of the preceding chapter is also taken into account. Let us assume that the rate of growth of the labour force $\beta = 1.5$ per cent per annum; that of labour productivity $\alpha = 5.5$ per cent; and consequently, that of the national income in the initial situation $r_0 = 7$ per cent. Suppose that by taking advantage of a labour reserve the rate of growth of the national income is raised to the level $r = 8$ per cent. This, however, is done gradually, so as to maintain real wages at a constant level throughout the transition period. Suppose, furthermore, that in the initial period the relative share of productive accumulation in the national

37

income, $i_0 = 26$ per cent. In order to raise r to the level of 8 per cent per annum it is necessary to increase this share to 29 per cent (which corresponds to a capital–output ratio $k = 3$). From formula (20) we then obtain

$$\tau = \log\frac{0.74}{0.71}\cdot\frac{1}{0.055} = 0.8 \text{ years}$$

During this period the average annual rate of growth is about 7.5 per cent. We assume that in the subsequent period of 3 years (in which the rate of growth is 8 per cent), the reserve is exhausted. Thus over the whole period the national income is increased in the proportion $(1.075)^{0.8}\cdot(1.08)^3 = 1.33$. If the rate of growth had been maintained at the initial level of $r = 7$ per cent, the national income would have been increased during the same period in the proportion $(1.07)^{3.8} = 1.28$. Hence, the absorption of excess labour permits an additional increase in the national income in the proportion $1.33/1.28 = 1.04$ – i.e. by 4 per cent. When the reserve has been absorbed and the rate of growth has returned to 7 per cent, the relative share of productive accumulation in the national income falls back to 26 per cent and that of consumption to 74 per cent (i.e. to the proportions which would have existed if the rate of growth had been maintained all the time at the initial level); the additional proportional increase in consumption as a result of this process is therefore equal to that in the national income – i.e. to 4 per cent.

2. It follows that the acceleration of growth for only a limited period brings an unquestionable advantage; but can it be treated as equivalent to a permanent increase in the rate of growth? The only possible reason for answering in the affirmative would be that when returning to the initial lower rate of growth, we go back at the same time to the original proportion between productive accumulation and consumption. This argument may, however, be countered as follows: even if there are no physical obstacles to the unlimited continuation of a higher rate of growth, this does not exclude the possibility of returning at any time to the initial rate, with a corresponding reduction in the

rate of productive accumulation. But if these obstacles do exist we *have* to return eventually to the initial position – unless we resort to mechanization which would require additional investment outlays (this will be discussed in more detail in a later chapter). Thus it will be seen that the case of raising the rate of growth from r_0 to r for a limited period must be treated as less favourable than raising this rate permanently.

We may thus say that an increase $r - r_0$ over a limited period could be expressed in terms of a permanent increase by means of a function $f(r - r_0)$, such that

$$f(r - r_0) < r - r_0$$

In addition the function has the following characteristics:

(*a*) When the value of r is r_0, the problem of exhausting the reserve does not arise, and hence $f(o) = o$.

(*b*) If $r - r_0$ is equal to a very small fraction, δ, the reserve will be exhausted after a very long period of time. This can be treated as equivalent to an unlimited period of time. Hence we have $f(\delta) = \delta$. Taking into account $f(o) = o$ we obtain

$$\frac{f(\delta) - f(o)}{\delta} = 1,$$

which means that the derivative of the function f is equal to 1 for $r = r_0$.

(*c*) Finally, we may assume that f is an increasing function, but that as $r - r_0$ increases the difference between $r - r_0$ and $f(r - r_0)$ also increases. Indeed, the higher $r - r_0$, the sooner is the given reserve of labour exhausted, and the greater the divergence between $r - r_0$ and $f(r - r_0)$; consequently the derivative of the function f is positive and the same is true of the derivative of the expression $(r - r_0) - f(r - r_0)$. Thus we have

$$\frac{\Delta f(r - r_0)}{\Delta r} > o$$

as well as

$$1 - \frac{\Delta f(r - r_0)}{\Delta r} > o$$

and hence

$$o < \frac{\Delta f(r - r_0)}{\Delta r} < 1$$

The inequality $\dfrac{\Delta f(r-r_0)}{\Delta r} < 1$

is not satisfied, however, in the case of $r = r_0$, since, as shown in point (b), we may disregard the exhaustion of the reserve when $r - r_0$ is very small, so that for $r = r_0$ the derivative is equal to 1. Thus we may finally write

$$\frac{\Delta f(r - r_0)}{\Delta r} = 1 \quad \text{for} \quad r = r_0$$

$$0 < \frac{\Delta f(r - r_0)}{\Delta r} < 1 \quad \text{for} \quad r > t_0$$

These results enable us now to consider the determination of the rate of growth where the reserve of labour is limited. In the case of an *unlimited* reserve the balance of advantages and disadvantages of increasing the rate of growth by Δr was expressed as follows

$$\Delta r - \frac{\omega(i)}{1 - i} \Delta i$$

Since in the case of a limited reserve the 'equivalent' of r is $r_0 + f(r - r_0)$, it follows that instead of Δr we must introduce $\Delta f(r - r_0)$ in this expression. We thus obtain

$$\Delta f(r - r_0) - \frac{\omega(i)}{1 - i} \Delta i$$

or

$$\frac{\Delta f(r - r_0)}{\Delta r} \Delta r \frac{\omega(i)}{1 - i} \Delta i$$

Hence the condition for determining the rate of growth of the national income will now be

$$\frac{\Delta r}{\Delta i} = \frac{\omega(i)}{(1 - i) \dfrac{\Delta f(r - r_0)}{\Delta r}}$$

whereas with unlimited labour it was

$$\frac{\Delta r}{\Delta i} = \frac{\omega(i)}{1 - i}.$$

Limited reserve of labour

In Fig. 5 the decision curve $D'K'$ represents the case where there are unlimited reserves of labour, its ordinates being determined by the expression $\omega(i)/(1-i)$. The decision curve $D'L'$ represents the case where there is a limited reserve of labour and its ordinates are determined by the expression

$$\frac{\omega(i)}{(1-i)\dfrac{\Delta f(r-r_0)}{\Delta r}}$$

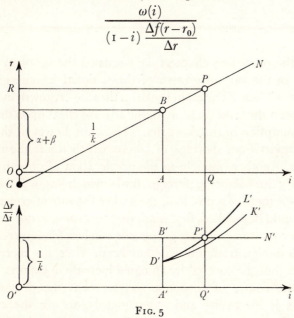

FIG. 5

Since $\Delta f(r-r_0)/\Delta r$ is equal to one for $r = r_0$ and less than one (but positive) for $r > r_0$, the two curves have a common point of departure, but they diverge, $D'L'$ being situated above $D'K'$.

As a result, the point of intersection of the 'decision curve' and the horizontal line, $B'N'$, is shifted to the left in the case of a limited reserve of labour. Thus in such a case the relative share of productive accumulation in the national income i and the rate of growth r tends to be fixed at a lower level than in the case of unlimited supplies of labour. This may be interpreted as the effect of the labour-supply barrier on the rate of growth; a limited reserve of labour only makes it possible to shift this barrier, not to eliminate it altogether.

6. BALANCING FOREIGN TRADE AS A FACTOR LIMITING THE RATE OF GROWTH

1. In the preceding chapters we discussed the problem of the choice of the rate of growth of the national income given a reserve of labour. The main brake on the rate of growth in such a situation is the 'cost' in terms of the adverse effect upon the level of consumption in the short run. This is not, however, the only factor apart from shortage of labour which limits the rate of growth. Another obstacle to the acceleration of growth is the difficulty in balancing foreign trade which – as will be seen below – is more of a problem, the higher the rate of growth.

It should be recalled, first of all, that according to our assumptions the economy neither grants nor receives foreign credits so that its foreign trade must be balanced. Thus any increase in imports must be covered by an equal increase in exports.

In the course of economic development the demand for imports is increasing and, consequently, so are the exports required to cover the imports. It follows that the higher the rate of growth of national income r, the more rapidly must exports increase and the more difficult it is to sell them, in view of the limited foreign demand for the products of a given country. A higher rate of growth r will thus require *ceteris paribus* a greater effort to promote exports or to restrict imports. Efforts to promote exports will be associated with reductions in export prices for certain goods in certain markets, with a shift to less profitable markets, and with the inclusion of less profitable items in the list of exportable goods. The effort to curtail imports consists, of course, of substituting home-made goods for imported commodities.

In all these cases the increase in the national income will tend

42

to decline in relation to the outlays of capital and labour involved. Indeed, if foreign trade is balanced, the national income is – according to our definitions – equal to the sum of productive accumulation and consumption (in the broad sense) at constant prices. But in the circumstances outlined above the outlays necessary to obtain certain commodities will increase – because the imports of these goods will either be paid for by a larger volume of exports, or by exports of a different structure requiring higher outlays, or because the outlays necessary to produce at home the commodities formerly imported will be higher than those for producing the exports by means of which they were procured.

As a result, efforts to maintain the rate of growth at a higher level will reduce the increment in the national income corresponding to given outlays and this reduction is greater the higher the level attained.

2. The phenomena described above emerge against the background of difficulties encountered in placing the exports which have to increase along with the rapidly growing national income in order to cover the cost of imports. This, however, is not the only source of difficulties in balancing foreign trade at a high rate of growth of national income. When this rate exceeds a certain level, the output of certain industries in the national economy – particularly those producing raw materials – lags behind the demand for those products owing to certain technological and organizational factors of which more will be said below. Hence, either the demand for imports of these products increases, or their export potential declines. The outcome is a gap in foreign trade which calls for appropriate efforts in promoting exports, or substituting home production for imports – again tending to reduce the increment in the national income corresponding to given outlays.

The technological and organizational factors limiting the rate of growth in particular industries are of varied character. The simplest case is that of limited natural resources (mineral deposits, woods, fisheries).

Moreover, experience in implementing plans for economic development shows that insurmountable difficulties arise whenever the expansion of a particular industry exceeds a certain rate, even if finance is adequate. An important role is played here by the long periods of construction of some projects, e.g. of coal mines.

Indeed, given the rate of expansion in a particular industry, the volume of 'projects under construction' is proportional to the length of the period of construction. If this period is long and the rate of expansion is high, the number of different 'building sites' becomes so great that the available technical and organizational staff is not adequate to run them efficiently. As a result, the period of construction becomes longer still, and the excessive number o 'building sites' leads to 'freezing' of capital rather than to a more rapid expansion of the industry concerned. It must be borne in mind that the technical and organizational staff required for the construction of plant has to be very highly skilled – much more so than the staff who will run the plant in the future.

Limited natural resources and the long period of construction are not, however, the only technical and organizational factors hampering the rate of expansion in individual sectors of the economy. One should also take into account the difficulty of recruiting workers to particular occupations (e.g. coal mining), and the time necessary to master new technological processes.

A specific case is that of agriculture where a certain element of spontaneity always remains in the development of production. In particular, the introduction of higher technology takes rather a long time here.

3. Let us now return to the influence of difficulties in balancing foreign trade on the rate of growth of the national income.

We again adopt as our initial situation the growth at a rate $r_0 = \alpha + \beta$, where α denotes the rate of increase in labour productivity resulting from technical progress, and β is the natural rate of growth of the labour force. In the case of an unlimited supply of labour the rate of growth of national income may be increased and for this purpose the rate of productive accumulation is raised from i_0 to i. If no difficulties in balancing foreign trade were caused by this acceleration, the rate of growth would rise from r_0 to a level ρ represented as a function of i by the ordinate of the line BN (see Fig. 6). The annual increment in national income Y would then be ρY; but it follows from the above that as a result of difficulties in balancing foreign trade, this increment will amount to $rY < \rho Y$. Thus the rate of growth r will be lower than ρ. In addition the higher i and ρ, the greater

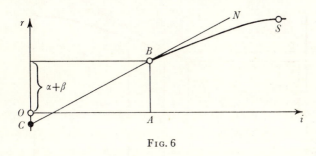

Fig. 6

are the difficulties with foreign trade, and the lower the ratio $(r-r_0)/(\rho-r_0)$. In Fig. 6, as was noted above, the straight line BN represents the relationship between ρ and i, while the relationship between r and i is now represented by the curve BS. It will be seen that on the diagram this curve levels off at the point S. This signifies that owing to the difficulties in foreign trade the rate r cannot exceed a certain level. Such is, indeed, the case in reality. At a certain rate of growth all efforts to equilibrate imports and exports cease to yield positive results. A further reduction in export prices does not serve any useful purpose, because it increases the volume of exports, but not its value (in foreign exchange) – the increase in volume being compensated by the decrease in price. Both less favourable markets and less profitable goods have been made use of to the limit. The same is true of feasible investment in import substitution. Thus foreign trade difficulties resulting from limited foreign markets, along with the technological and organizational factors which hamper the development of particular industries, set a ceiling for the rate of growth.

4. As indicated above, the difficulties experienced in foreign trade lead to an increase in the outlays of both capital and labour per unit increment in national income. As far as a higher labour outlay is concerned, this amounts to a relative reduction of productivity within the increment of national income (i.e. marginal productivity). This results in the rate of increase of

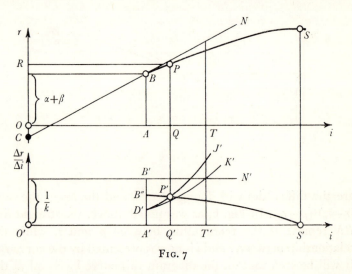

FIG. 7

average productivity falling short of the rate α produced by technical progress.†

As a result, the transition period τ, during which the rate of productive accumulation is raised from i_0 to i by keeping real wages stable despite increasing productivity of labour, is lengthened.

5. In Fig. 7 the determination of the rate of growth is presented in a similar way to that of Fig. 4. Since the slope of the tangent at

† If it is assumed that the marginal productivity of labour in the sense employed here remains constant over time, provided the effects of technical progress are eliminated, and if, moreover, it is assumed as above that this productivity is lower than average productivity in the economy in the initial period calculated on the basis of the new technique in that period – then it is clear that the rate of increase in average productivity differs less and less from α, approaching this level asymptotically.

any point of the curve *BS* is lower than that of the straight line *BN*, the curve *B″S′* representing $\Delta r/\Delta i$ is situated below the line *B′N′* which corresponds to the slope $1/k$. Moreover, since the slope of the curve *BS* diminishes as i rises, reaching the zero at point *S*, the curve *B″S′* is downward-sloping and intersects the i-axis at the point *S′*, vertically below point *S*.

The curve *D′J′* is a 'government decision curve' conceptually identical to the curve *D′K′* in Fig. 4. However, the latter needs some modification as a result of difficulties in balancing foreign trade. As pointed out above, the transition period τ, during which the rate of productive accumulation is raised from i_0 to i with real wages remaining stable, is lengthened as a result of difficulties in balancing foreign trade; as a result the coefficient $\omega(i)$ is increased in the expression representing the balance of advantages and disadvantages of raising the rate of growth, i.e.

$$\Delta r - \frac{\omega(i)}{1-i}\Delta i$$

This reflects the fact that the conditions for raising the relative share of accumulation i in the national income deteriorate and thus the 'cost' of increasing i by Δi increases. As a result the appropriate 'decision curve' *D′J′* is above the curve *D′K′* which does not allow for the effect of difficulties in balancing foreign trade upon attempts to raise the rate of growth.

As in Fig. 4, the rate of productive accumulation and the rate of growth of the national income are determined by the point of intersection *P′* of the curves *D′J′* and *B″S′*, which is projected onto the curve *BS*. If difficulties in foreign trade are disregarded, i and r are determined by the point of intersection of the horizontal line *B′N′* and the curve *D′K′*, which is projected onto the straight line *BN*. It will be seen that difficulties in balancing foreign trade lead to the adoption of a much lower rate of growth; firstly, the rate of productive accumulation is fixed by the government at a level *OQ* which is lower than *OT*; and secondly, the point *P* corresponding to it lies on the curve *BS* which is situated below the straight line *BN*.

47

6. It is quite possible that B'', the point of departure of the curve $B''S'$, may be identical with D', the beginning of the decision curve. This would, of course, mean that the government should not raise the rate of growth above the level $r_0 = \alpha + \beta$, i.e. that determined by the rate of increase in productivity of labour resulting from technical progress and natural growth of the labour force.

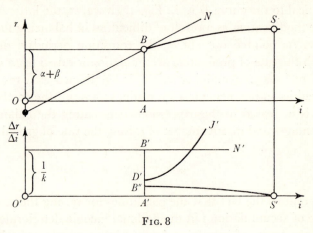

FIG. 8

It is also conceivable that point B'' will lie below D' (see Fig. 8). Would this mean that the government would slow down the rate of growth below the level r_0?

Since it may be assumed that the government is unwilling to accept growing unemployment, it can be assumed that the 'decision curve' drops abruptly to the left of point D', so that the curves $B''S'$ and $D'J'$ intersect practically at point B'' and thus the rate of growth is equal to r_0.

It is obvious that the situation considered here, where it is decided not to raise the rate of growth above $r_0 = \alpha + \beta$, may also arise without difficulties in balancing foreign trade. However, these difficulties make it much more likely, since they contribute to the curve $B''S'$ being situated below the straight line $B'N'$.

7. Let us now introduce the problem of a limited reserve of labour. The curve BS, and hence the curve $B''S'$, will not be

affected. The fact that the reserve of labour is limited will be reflected – as in our argument in the preceding chapter – in the position of the 'decision curve' $D'I'$ (see Fig. 9) which has a common point of departure with the 'decision curve' for an unlimited reserve of labour $D'J'$, but for values of i higher than i_0 is situated above the latter. Foreign trade difficulties tend to

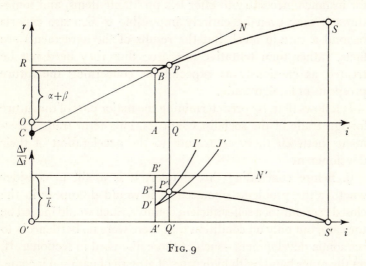

FIG. 9

shift the curve even further, since they result in a more rapid absorption of the labour reserve owing to the reduction in the rate of increase of the productivity of labour (see section 4 of the present chapter).

The rate of growth of national income is given by the point P' at the intersection of the curves $B''S'$ and $D'I'$. It is, of course, lower than the rate of growth with an unlimited labour reserve, which is determined by the point of intersection of the curves $B''S'$ and $D'J'$.

8. It should be noted that in long-run plans the estimation of the impact of foreign trade on the increment in national income which corresponds to given outlays is always very hypothetical in character. Thus uncertainty will lead to the adoption of rather 'conservative' estimates and thus ultimately to the choice of a

4   49

relatively low rate of growth. Therefore the elimination of this uncertainty by long-term trade agreements, such as are concluded within the socialist camp – favours a higher rate of growth of national income. Obviously, such agreements do not solve the problem of placing the increased exports. When the other party is not willing to accept larger quantities of certain commodities it is, for instance, necessary to offer less profitable items, and sometimes it may even be entirely impossible to increase exports beyond a certain level. But the results of the agreements are facts, rather than tentative forecasts; thus they need not be treated as cautiously as expectations concerning the future prospects of foreign trade.

It follows that, by predetermining the major part of the future foreign trade of the socialist countries, long-term trade agreements between them contribute to the acceleration of their development.

9. Before concluding this chapter, it is useful to consider whether the problems discussed in it would disappear in the closed economy of a self-sufficient country. Such would indeed be the case, but only on condition that there were no bottlenecks to economic development – such as those discussed in section 2. If, on the other hand, with high rates of growth of national income, the output of particular industries lagged behind demand due to the influence of technological and organizational factors, then the factors hampering development would be further accentuated in the absence of foreign trade. Indeed, there would be then no possibility of filling the gaps by imports acquired in exchange for exports of those goods whose production can expand without encountering technological and organizational barriers. The only possible approach to the long-run bottlenecks would be to produce substitutes for the scarce goods (corresponding to the substitution of home production for imports discussed in preceding sections) which in many cases would be much less favourable than the expansion of exports.

7. ACCELERATION OF THE INCREASE IN LABOUR PRODUCTIVITY BY RAISING THE CAPITAL–OUTPUT RATIO OR BY SHORTENING THE LIFE-SPAN OF EQUIPMENT

1. In Chapters 4 and 5 we discussed the case in which the existence of a reserve of labour made it possible to increase the rate of growth, with the parameters m, k, a and u remaining constant. We shall now assume that in the initial situation we have no underemployment. Since the rate of increase of the labour force is treated as given, the acceleration of growth in such a case may be achieved only by raising the rate of increase of labour productivity. This may be done by changing one of the above parameters as follows:

(*a*) increasing the capital–output ratio m and thus also the parameter k;†

(*b*) shortening the life-span of equipment, which leads to an increase in the parameter of depreciation a.

We shall begin by considering the effects of increasing the capital–output ratio. In order to prepare the ground for this discussion we have first briefly to examine the problem of the 'production curve' and that of technical progress.

2. Let us consider the problem of different ways of producing an increment in the national income using new investment. Let us assume that this increment has a given structure – in other words, it consists of given quantities of various final products (i.e. products that do not go through further manufacturing

† Let us recall that m is the capital–output ratio for fixed capital only, and k is the ratio for fixed capital together with inventories.

processes within the period considered). Usually, each of these products, or rather group of similar products, can be produced by several different methods of production based on technical knowledge existing at a given time. It follows that to produce a given increment in the national income there exists an immense number of variants, each of them consisting of a combination of variants for producing particular types of commodity. Let us denote by s the number of types of commodity, by N_1 the number of variants for the first group of products, by N_2 the number of those for the second type ... and by N_s the number of those for the sth type. The total number of combinations for all types of commodity will then be $N_1 . N_2 . N_3 ..... N_s$ which for a large s will be a very large number, even if we only have two alternatives for each type of commodity.

When production is considered in all its stages, each variant is characterized by specific outlays of investment and labour. Out of all the possible variants for producing a given increment in the national income, we may discard those which are 'worse' than some others, with respect to both investment and labour inputs – i.e. which require higher outlays of both factors (or an equal outlay of one and a higher outlay of the other), i.e. variants which are absolutely inferior. We shall then be left with only those variants where greater investment is associated with less labour and vice versa. These may be represented diagrammatically as in Fig. 10.

As the abscissa we plot investment outlay and as the ordinate the labour outlay required to produce a given increment in the national income. Each variant will then be represented by a different point on the curve. It is clear that the set of admissible variants may be represented by a downward sloping curve such as MN. Indeed, to any given investment outlay OA there corresponds only one labour outlay AB. If there were two possible corresponding values of the labour outlay, then the alternative involving the higher outlay of labour would be less favourable and would be rejected. The curve is downwards sloping, since – as was pointed out – a higher investment outlay is associated with a lower outlay of labour. The curve MN is called the 'production curve'.†

If this curve refers to a unit increment in the national income, the investment outlay is equal to the capital–output ratio m, the latter being simply the investment outlay per unit increment in national income (see Chapter 2, section 1). Let us denote the labour outlay per unit increment in national income by λ. Accordingly, we shall plot m on the abscissa and λ on the ordinate (see Fig. 11).

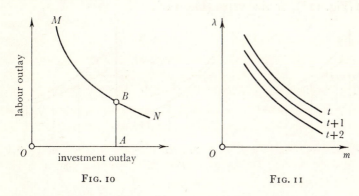

FIG. 10   FIG. 11

The curve of production at time t is – as mentioned above – based on the body of technical knowledge existing at that time as a result of previous technical progress. But technical progress does not stop at time t, and is reflected in a downward shift of the curve of production which takes the successive positions $t + 1$, $t + 2$, etc. Thus, owing to technical progress, the λ corresponding to a given m is subject to a steady decline. We shall call technical progress 'uniform' if the labour outlay λ corresponding to a given m decreases at a constant rate. This means that with a constant level of the capital–output ratio m, the productivity of

† It may seem doubtful whether the central authorities are able to check on the multitude of variants in order to eliminate those which are absolutely inferior to some alternative variant. It is possible to show, however, that if in particular branches of the economy the choice between alternative variants is based on the evaluation of the efficiency of investment, these variants are automatically eliminated (see Appendix at the end of Part I, p. 112 from which it also follows that the curve of production is concave).

labour in new plant increases at a constant rate. It is this case that was considered in the previous chapters.

From the fact that to a given m there corresponds a fixed rate of decrease in the unit labour outlay λ, and thus also a definite rate of increase of productivity, it does not necessarily follow that this rate is the same for all values of the capital–output ratio m. Such a case is represented in Fig. 12 a, and is possible but not inevitable. It is conceivable that the rate of decrease of λ (or the rate of increase in productivity) is greater the higher the value of m (Fig. 12 b), or vice versa (Fig. 12 c).

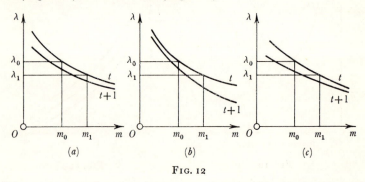

Fig. 12

In case (a) a shift towards higher capital intensity (from m_0 to m_1) causes a once-for-all increase in productivity in new plant, but does not raise the *rate* of increase of this productivity; we describe such technical progress as 'neutral'. In case (b) the rate of increase in productivity is greater the greater capital intensity; we describe this type of technical progress as 'encouraging capital intensity'. Finally, in case (c) a rise in capital intensity, while bringing about an increase in the level of productivity in new plant, leads at the same time to a decline in the rate of increase in labour productivity. Accordingly, this type of technical progress will be described as 'discouraging capital intensity'.

We may give the following example of technical progress 'encouraging capital intensity'. Suppose there are two variants for each group of products: A of a lower, and B of a higher capital intensity. Suppose, moreover, that in newly invented variants

54

the capital intensity is in all cases equal to that of *B*. The level of productivity is, of course, higher in those newly invented variants, so that all former variants *B* for individual groups of products must be discarded and replaced by newly discovered solutions. But there is no *a priori* reason for discarding the variants *A*, because their capital intensity is lower than that of the new solutions.

Let us consider the repercussions of this type of technical progress if *m* is given. At time *t* there corresponds to a given *m* a definite combination of variants for individual groups of products: in some cases it is the variant *A* and in others *B*. At time *t* + 1, according to what we said above, in all cases where new inventions have occurred, the variants *B* will have been replaced by newly invented solutions. But, if *m* is to stay constant, the variants *A* must not be touched since, should they be replaced by newly invented variants of capital intensity *B*, *m* would have to change. It is now easy to see that technical progress is here 'encouraging capital intensity'. Indeed, the higher the value of *m*, the greater the weight of more capital-intensive variants *B*, and thus the greater the scope for replacement by newly discovered solutions, and the greater the increase in productivity.

For technical progress 'discouraging capital intensity', the following situation may be given as an example. Let us suppose that the newly invented variants have a capital intensity equal to that of the variants *A* and that their level of productivity, though increasing, remains below that of the variants *B* in the years considered. It follows that whenever a new invention occurs the variants *A* must be discarded and replaced by the newly discovered techniques. But there is no *a priori* reason for the variants *B* to be discarded, since by assumption they have a higher productivity than the new inventions. By time *t* + 1, therefore, the combination of variants for individual products which corresponded to a given *m* at time *t* has been changed by replacing variants *A* by newly discovered techniques, leaving variants *B* unaltered; if variants *B* were to be replaced by new techniques of the capital intensity of *A*, *m* would have to change.

The higher the value of m the smaller the weight of less capital intensive variants; consequently, there is less scope for replacement by newly discovered techniques and the increase in productivity is smaller. Thus this is a case of technical progress 'discouraging capital intensity'.

3. The prevailing type of technical progress by no means dictates the path economic development takes in practice. For example, if technical progress is 'encouraging capital intensity', this does not mean that the coefficient m is bound to increase. It follows from Fig. 12 *b* that in such a case even when m remains constant we shall obtain a regular increase in productivity in the new plant. By contrast, in the case of neutral technical progress there is no necessity for m to remain constant; we may raise it gradually and in this way achieve a more rapid increase in productivity by moving to the right along the curve of production as it shifts downwards. Obviously, such an operation is much more attractive when technical progress is 'encouraging capital intensity' because then we gain also the advantage of a higher rate of increase in productivity for higher capital–output ratios.

In what follows we shall concentrate on a detailed discussion of the effects of a once-for-all increase in the capital–output ratio, this being a more elementary case than that of its continuous increase. Our analysis also sheds some light on the latter more complicated case which will, however, be treated only in a general way.

4. We shall now examine the repercussions of raising the capital–output ratio on the increase in the average productivity of labour. Let us first take the case of neutral technical progress. If at time t the capital–output ratio is raised from m_0 to m_1, this involves a rise in productivity which is proportional to the reciprocal of the relative decline in the quantity of labour required – i.e. a rise in the proportion λ_0/λ_1 (see Fig. 12 *a*). This obviously applies to labour productivity in new plant. As far as aggregate capital equipment is concerned, adjustment to a higher capital–output ratio is carried out gradually. Every year some equipment based on the 'old' technology (corresponding

to m_0) is scrapped, and some new equipment based on the 'new' technology (corresponding to m_1) is added. The longer this process goes on, the greater becomes the 'recast' portion of total capital equipment. Finally, after a period n, equal to the life-span of equipment – i.e. after the complete elimination of equipment characterized by the 'old' technique – all the fixed capital has a capital–output ratio m_1 and labour productivity is correspondingly higher. Thus the rise in productivity which is realized immediately for new plant takes a period of n years to extend to aggregate fixed capital.

During this period average productivity increases at a higher rate than that resulting from technical progress. (The latter rate remains unchanged after the capital–output ratio has been raised from m_0 to m_1, since we are here discussing neutral technical progress.) The labour released from scrapping old plant, and the newly accruing labour force, produces a higher output than if m had not been increased. Thus the increment in the national income due to new investment is raised while the loss of national income resulting from discarding old equipment remains unchanged. The difference between the rate of increase of productivity and α is greatest at the beginning of the period of 'recasting'; as the higher capital–output ratio and higher productivity pervade the stock of capital equipment more and more, new investment contributes proportionately less to the increase of both the overall capital–output ratio and overall productivity, because the difference between new investment and the stock of capital equipment is less and less pronounced. Eventually, when all fixed capital is 'recast' the process of raising the rate of increase of labour productivity comes to an end. Indeed, at this point the two following conditions hold:

(*a*) the whole stock of equipment is characterized by the same capital intensity and productivity as new investment;

(*b*) the loss of national income due to scrapping of obsolete equipment is also increased accordingly. Thus the rate of increase of productivity goes back to its normal level – resulting solely from technical progress – and the rate of growth of the

A socialist economy

national income to the level $\alpha + \beta$. The changes in the rate of
growth of national income and in productivity in the period of
'recasting' are represented in Fig. 13, where δ denotes the increment in the rate of increase of productivity at the beginning of
that period. The rate of increase of productivity (shaded area)
declines over the period of 'recasting' from $\alpha + \delta$ to α, and the
rate of growth of the national income from $\alpha + \delta + \beta$ to $\alpha + \beta$. The
abrupt drop in these rates at the end of 'recasting' reflects the

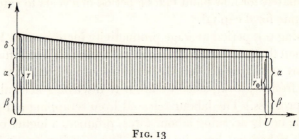

Fig. 13

fact that the equipment scrapped begins also to be endowed with
higher productivity of labour.

This process will follow a different course in the case of
technical progress 'encouraging capital intensity'. In this case,
the adoption of a higher capital–output ratio results not only in a
once-for-all increase in productivity in the new plant, but also in
an increased rate of growth of this productivity. Thus when the
process of 'recasting' to give the stock of capital equipment a
higher capital intensity comes to an end after n years, the rate of
growth of productivity does not go back to the initial level α, but
is stabilized at a higher level α'. During the period of 'recasting'
the slackening of the pace at which fixed capital is adjusted to a
higher capital intensity – and consequently to a higher labour
productivity – is, at least in part, compensated by the increasing
influence of the rise in productivity in the new plant at a rate α',
greater than α.

5. Let us consider now the problem of increasing productivity
by shortening the life-span of equipment. The shorter this life-
span, the higher is the average productivity of labour, because

58

this average is then nearer to the level of productivity in new plant. In other words, the lower the average age of the stock of capital equipment, the higher the average productivity of labour.

Suppose, now, that the life-span of equipment is initially n. The 'rejuvenation' of fixed capital by a gradual reduction in the life-span of equipment to n' will lead, according to the above, to an increase in the average productivity of labour. But after this increase has been effected the rate of growth of productivity will fall back to the initial level α, and that of the national income to $\alpha + \beta$. This is similar to what happened in the case of 'recasting' fixed capital in order to raise its intensity with neutral technical progress; there too, after aggregate fixed capital has been endowed with a higher capital intensity the rate of increase in productivity falls back to the initial level.

The 'rejuvenation' of fixed capital is assumed to be carried out by increasing the scrapping of productive capacity in the proportion a/a_0 where the parameter of depreciation a_0 corresponds to the life-span n and to the constant rate of growth $r_0 = \alpha + \beta$, while the parameter a corresponds to a shorter life-span n' and the same rate of growth.

It may be shown that after n' years the equipment existing at the outset of the 'rejuvenation' will have been scrapped, and thus the process of 'rejuvenation' will then be complete.† Moreover, the actual parameter of depreciation is obviously nearly equal to a in the first year of the 'rejuvenation' process, since the national

† Let us denote the productive capacities which in the initial position correspond to investment in the previous n years – i.e. to $I_1, I_2, ..., I_n$ – by $P_1, P_2, ..., P_n$. P is not proportional to I because of the factor u (see Chapter 3, section 2). Aggregate productive capacity existing at that time is therefore equal to $P_1 + P_2 + ... + P_n$. Thus in the absence of 'rejuvenation' the capacities scrapped in the subsequent n years would be $P_1, P_2, ...$ etc. Multiplying these quantities by the factor a/a_0 we obtain $P_1(a/a_0), P_2(a/a_0), ...$ etc. for the capacities existing in the initial position scrapped in successive years. But from section 2 of Chapter 3 it follows that for uniform growth

$$\frac{a}{a_0} = \frac{P_1 + P_2 + ... + P_n}{P_1 + P_2 + ... + P_{n'}}.$$

Thus in the course of n' years the aggregate productive capacity existing in the initial position will have been scrapped:

$$(P_1 + P_2 + ... + P_{n'}) \frac{P_1 + P_2 + ... + P_n}{P_1 + P_2 + ... + P_{n'}} = P_1 + P_2 + ... + P_n.$$

income still differs little from what it would be without 'rejuvenation', while the loss of output due to the scrapping of old capacities is increased in the proportion a/a_0. Finally it may be shown rigorously that after the termination of the 'rejuvenation' process the system returns to uniform growth at a rate r_0 with a parameter of depreciation a.‡

‡ Let us first suppose that there is no attempt at 'rejuvenation', and the process of uniform growth at a rate r_0 continues for n years. We denote the capacity at the end of the period created by new investment in successive years of that period by Q_1, Q_2, ..., Q_n. It is clear that $Q_1 = P_1(1+r_0)^n$; $Q_2 = P_2(1+r_0)^n$; ... etc. where P_1, P_2, ... etc. have the same meaning as in the previous footnote. Now the capacity Q_1 may be divided into two parts: that manned by the labour released by the scrapping of the capacity P_1, and secondly, that manned by new additions to the labour force (including that resulting from the discrepancy between the rate of increase in productivity in existing plant w and the rate of improvement in the utilization of equipment u — cf. note †, p. 23. The first part will be $P_1(1+\alpha)^n$ and the second

$$Q_1 - P_1(1+\alpha)^n; \quad \text{or} \quad \frac{Q_1}{(1+r_0)^n}(1+\alpha)^n = \frac{Q_1}{(1+\beta)^n}, \quad \text{and} \quad Q_1 - \frac{Q_1}{(1+\beta)^n}$$

respectively. Let us now increase the scrapping of old productive capacity in the proportion a/a_0. As a result the labour released by scrapping will be increased in this proportion. The productive capacity corresponding to Q_1 will be higher now because the second component remains unchanged but the first becomes

$$\frac{Q_1}{(1+\beta)^n}\frac{a}{a_0}$$

Thus total capacity will be

$$\frac{Q_1}{(1+\beta)^n}\frac{a}{a_0} + \left[Q_1 - \frac{Q_1}{(1+\beta)^n}\right] = Q_1\left[\left(\frac{a}{a_0}-1\right)\frac{1}{(1+\beta)^n}+1\right]$$

This, however, is the productive capacity as it would exist after n years. In fact, the process of 'rejuvenation' is terminated according to the preceding footnote after n' years. Thus the capacity as it will exist at the time of termination of the process will be reduced in the proportion

$$\frac{1}{(1+u)^{n-n'}}.$$

Consequently it will amount to

$$Q_1' = Q_1\frac{\left(\dfrac{a}{a_0}-1\right)\dfrac{1}{(1+\beta)^n}+1}{(1+u)^{n-n'}}$$

A similar expression will be obtained for the capacities Q_2', Q_3', ..., $Q_{n'}'$. It follows that in the process of 'rejuvenation' all the productive capacities Q_1, Q_2, ..., $Q_{n'}$ are raised in the same proportion while the capacities

$$P_1(a/a_0), \quad P_2(a/a_0), \quad ..., \quad P_{n'}(a/a_0)$$

are scrapped instead of P_1, P_2, ..., $P_{n'}$. From this it is easy to conclude that after the period of 'rejuvenation' the system is poised for uniform growth at a rate r_0, the life-span of equipment being n' and the parameter of depreciation a.

8. INCREASING THE RATE OF GROWTH OF NATIONAL INCOME UNDER CONDITIONS OF FULL EMPLOYMENT BY RAISING THE CAPITAL–OUTPUT RATIO

1. Let us assume that labour productivity is increased by raising the capital–output ratio, technical progress being neutral. As a result of increasing the capital–output ratio from its initial level m_0 to the level m, labour productivity in new plant is raised $(1+p)$ times. As was pointed out above, for aggregate capital equipment this process of 'recasting' takes n years, where n is the life-span of equipment. During this period the average productivity of labour increases more rapidly than in the initial situation – i.e. at a rate higher than α. This extra growth, however, slackens gradually and comes to an end when the process of 'recasting' fixed capital is complete. The rate of increase in employment β being constant, this amounts to a faster growth of national income for a period of n years. The rate of growth, which was $r_0 = \alpha + \beta$ in the initial situation, is raised to the level $r = \alpha + \delta + \beta$ at the beginning of the period and declines back to $r_0 = \alpha + \beta$ at its end. Thus it is obvious that the average rate of growth of the national income over the period of 'recasting' is higher than r_0, but lower than r. It amounts to:

$$r_{av} = (1+r_0)\sqrt[n]{(1+p)} - 1 \qquad (21)$$

For at the end of n years the national income will be

$$(1+r_0)^n (1+p)$$

times its level in the initial year, since the productivity of labour is increased $(1+p)$ times by the increase in capital intensity.†

† This can be proved rigorously as follows: the labour released by scrapping old plant, and by new accruals to the labour force (including that resulting from the

Thus on the average, the national income will increase in the proportion $(1 + r_0) \sqrt[n]{(1 + p)}$ each year, and its average annual rate of growth will be $(1 + r_0) \sqrt[n]{(1 + p)} - 1$.

We shall now present diagrammatically the process of accelerating the growth of national income. For this purpose we shall use a diagram similar to that in Fig. 2, p. 28. Again we plot the rate of productive accumulation i on the abscissa, and the rate of growth r of the national income on the ordinate. In the initial situation the rate of growth of the national income r_0 is equal to $\alpha + \beta$, while the capital–output ratio is k_0. The relationship between r and the rate of productive accumulation is expressed by the equation

$$r = \frac{1}{k_0} i - \frac{m_0}{k_0} (a - u) \tag{7'}$$

This equation is represented in Fig. 14 by the line BN, the slope of which is $1/k_0$. The rate of productive accumulation in the initial situation is i_0, equal to OA.

We now raise the capital–output ratio from its initial level m_0 to the level m. This results in a rise in the productivity of labour in new plant in the proportion $1 + p$. The capital–output ratio k_0 (which relates productive investment plus the increase in inventories to the increment in national income) is raised to the level k. We have

$$k - m = k_0 - m_0 = \mu \tag{22}$$

where μ is the coefficient showing the relation between the increase in inventories and that in national income (see Chapter 2, section 4). The relation between r and i in the new situation is expressed by the formula

$$r = \frac{1}{k} i - \frac{m}{k} (a - u) \tag{7}$$

discrepancy between the rate of increase in productivity in new plant, w, and the rate of improvement in the utilization of equipment, u (cf. note †, p. 23)) is the same as it would be if m remained unchanged. Hence now investment generates an output which is $(1 + p)$ times higher than in that case. Thus the aggregate stock of capital after the completion of 'recasting' produces an output which is increased in this proportion. It also follows that after the completion of 'recasting' the system is poised for uniform growth at a rate $\alpha + \beta$.

represented in the diagram by the straight line WV, the slope of which is $1/k$. We now determine F, the point of intersection of the straight lines BN and WV, by finding the solutions for r and i from equations (7′) and (7) while taking into account equation (22). We obtain $-\mu(a-u)$ for the abscissa of point F and $-(a-u)$ for the ordinate. It follows that the position of point F does not depend on the magnitude of the capital–output ratio, so that when k changes the straight line representing the relationship between r and i rotates around point F.

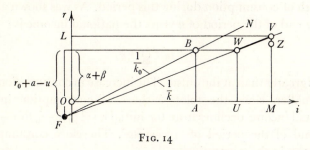

FIG. 14

As a result of raising the productivity of labour in new plant in the proportion $1+p$, the rate of growth of the national income in the first year of 'recasting' is increased to the level r represented by OL in Fig. 14. This is accompanied by a rise in the rate of productive accumulation to the level i, equal to OM. In the course of 'recasting' fixed capital, the point corresponding to the rate of growth and the rate of productive accumulation moves from V to W.† The point W shows the situation at the end

† It should be noted that the presentation of the process of 'recasting' by means of Fig. 14 is not quite accurate. The point F is not in fact fully immobile in the course of this process, since the parameter of depreciation does not remain unaltered during the 'recasting'. This would be the case if the rate of growth of the national income amounted to r_0 all the time. However, the whole aim of the process of 'recasting' is just to raise this rate. As a result the same volume of scrapping of old equipment (corresponding to its life-span n) will be associated with a higher level of national income than that which would obtain if the rate of growth r_0 had been maintained. Thus in the course of 'recasting' the parameter of depreciation a will be falling, and the point F will be moving upwards and to the right because its abscissa is $-\mu(a-u)$ and its ordinate $-(a-u)$.) As a result, in the period of 'recasting' the straight line FV will be shifting upwards, but without changing its slope. (We assume here that $\mu < 1$ which is quite realistic.) After this period there will be a return to the position FV shown in Fig. 14.

A socialist economy

of the period of 'recasting'. It is characterized by the initial rate of growth r_0 and the rate of accumulation i_n (equal to OU) which is higher than the rate of accumulation in the initial position, i_0 (equal to OA) owing to the higher capital–output ratio. The rate of growth falls back to its initial level, but the rise in the capital–output ratio is irreversible and burdens the economy 'for good' with a higher rate of productive accumulation.

This obviously affects the level of consumption at the end of the period of 'recasting' and, consequently, the average rate of growth of consumption during this period. As was shown above at the end of the period of n years the national income is

$$(1+r_0)^n (1+p)$$

times greater than at the outset. The increase in consumption will be smaller, since the relative share of consumption in the national income declines from the initial level of $1 - i_0$ to $1 - i_n$ at the end of the period of 'recasting'. Therefore consumption increases in the proportion

$$(1+r_0)^n (1+p) \frac{1 - i_n}{1 - i_0}$$

and its total 'extra growth' resulting from the 'recasting' of fixed capital, will be

$$(1+p) \frac{1 - i_n}{1 - i_0} \tag{23}$$

Since in the latter expression the first factor is greater and the second smaller than one, it cannot be taken for granted that the product exceeds 1. But if it does not, there is no sense in embarking upon the process of 'recasting' – i.e. on raising the capital intensity of the aggregate productive capacity. We shall see that the result of such a 'recasting' depends on the effect of the increase in capital intensity on the productivity of labour. Expression (23) may be rewritten in the form

$$(1+p) \left(1 - \frac{i_n - i_0}{1 - i_0}\right)$$

Now $i_n - i_0$ is equal to AU in Fig. 14 which in turn is equal to

$$BW = (r_0 + a - u)(k - k_0)$$

Consequently, the raising of the capital–output ratio is justified only if the condition

$$(1+p)\frac{1-i_n}{1-i_0} = (1+p)\left(1 - \frac{(r_0+a-u)(k-k_0)}{1-i_0}\right) > 1 \quad (23')$$

is fulfilled. The increase in consumption will be greater, the greater is the rise in p which results from raising the capital–output ratio from k_0 to k. If the response of the productivity of labour to the rise in capital intensity is weak, the condition $(23')$ is not fulfilled – i.e. there is no increase in consumption.

The average rate of growth of consumption is

$$c = (1+r_0)\sqrt[n]{(1+p)}\sqrt[n]{\left(\frac{1-i_n}{1-i_0}\right)} - 1 = (1+r_{\text{av}})\sqrt[n]{\left(\frac{1-i_n}{1-i_0}\right)} - 1 \quad (24)$$

and is obviously lower than the average rate of growth of the national income. But the latter rate is, according to the above argument, lower than r, i.e. the rate of growth of the national income at the beginning of the period of 'recasting'. Hence we have

$$r > c$$

which means that, during the period of 'recasting', consumption rises on average less rapidly than the national income at the beginning of this period.

This fact has much relevance for the decision as to how far it is desirable to accelerate the growth of national income by means of raising the capital–output ratio. For at the expense of increasing the rate of accumulation by $i - i_0 = AM$ (see Fig. 14) at the outset of the 'recasting' period we obtain an average rate of growth of consumption during this period $c = MZ$ which is lower than $r = MV$ but (according to our assumption about the purpose of 'recasting') higher than r_0 – i.e. an 'additional' increase in consumption over n years at an average rate of $c - r_0$.

2. This situation is roughly comparable with that described below arising in the case of unlimited supply of labour. Suppose that in the latter situation the level of the capital–output ratio is such that in order to raise the rate of growth of national income from r_0 to c, i.e. by $c - r_0$ it is necessary to increase the rate of productive accumulation by $i - i_0 = AM$. Suppose, moreover, that after n years we go back to the rate of growth $r_0 = \alpha + \beta$ and thus to the rate of accumulation i_0. Since the relative share of consumption in the national income before the period of accelerated growth and after n years is $1 - i_0$, the increase in consumption from the beginning of the period until the falling back of the rate of growth to r_0 is proportional to the change in the national income. Consequently the average rate of increase in consumption over the n-year period is $c > r_0$.† Thus as in the period of 'recasting' considered above the average rate of growth of consumption over the period of n years is increased by $c - r_0$ at the expense of raising the rate of accumulation by $i - i_0$ at the start of the process.

In the subsequent discussion of the choice of the capital–output ratio we shall, on the basis of this analogy, take into consideration the rate of accumulation i conjointly with the average rate of increase in consumption during the 'recasting' period rather than with the rate of growth of the national income at the beginning of this period, and as a first approximation we apply the same decision curve as in the case of an unlimited reserve of labour.‡

† In fact the course of the process is as follows: consumption falls at the beginning of this period in the proportion $(1-i)/(1-i_0)$. Next the national income and consumption grow for n years at a rate c (consumption bearing a constant relation $(1-i)$ to national income). Finally, after n years when the rate of growth falls back to r_0, consumption increases in the proportion $(1-i_0)/(1-i)$.

‡ The application of the same decision curve as in the case of unlimited labour supply is subject to some qualifications. First, in the latter case growth at a rate c may be continued indefinitely while in the case presently considered it may be continued for n years only. (It should be recalled, however, that n is a relatively long period of the order of 20 years.)

A second deficiency in the analogy works in the opposite direction. In the case of an unlimited reserve of labour the fall in the rate of productive accumulation occurs not earlier than at the very end of the period of n years, while in the present case this rate is decreasing throughout. It follows that, although the total increase in

3. In order to solve the problem whether and to what extent it is desirable to increase the capital intensity of the aggregate productive capacity we may use a similar method to that developed in Chapter 4 for dealing with the problem of increasing the rate of growth in the case of an unlimited reserve of labour. Let us first take points V and Z in Fig. 14 corresponding to different values of the capital–output ratio k. We shall then obtain two curves: BV and BZ (see Fig. 15). The former represents the relationship between the rate of productive accumulation i and the rate of growth of the national income r at the beginning of the period of 'recasting' n; the latter shows the relationship between the same rate of productive accumulation and the average rate of growth of consumption over the period of 'recasting'. The slope of the straight line joining a point on the curve BV with the point F is equal to the reciprocal of the capital–output ratio.

It should be noticed that the curve BZ reaches a maximum at point S and falls thereafter. The 'additional' relative increase in consumption during the period of 'recasting' amounts according to formula (23') to

$$(1+p)\frac{1-i_n}{1-i_0} = (1+p)\left[1 - \frac{(r_0+a-u)(k-k_0)}{1-i_0}\right]$$

Now, if k is sufficiently high the second factor on the right-hand side of the equation may even approach zero. This means that for a sufficiently large k, c must be negative, i.e. the curve BZ

consumption for the whole period of 'recasting' is the same in both cases, the shape of the time-curve of consumption within the period is more advantageous in the case presently considered. A further influence in the same direction is exerted by the rate of growth of national income being higher at the beginning of the period of 'recasting' than the average over the whole period. Thus, the case of 'recasting' of fixed capital in n years, when compared to the case of uniform growth (with the rate of growth falling back at the end of this period to its initial level of r_0 and the rate of productive accumulation returning, accordingly, to i_0), has the advantage of an earlier improvement in consumption. At the beginning of the period both processes are similar in that the share of consumption declines in both cases from $1-i_0$ to $1-i$. At the end of the period they again become identical with respect to the level of consumption achieved. But in the mid-period the former case gains a clear advantage over the latter.

We ignore these complications below.

intersects the i-axis and thus it reaches a maximum at some point S. It is clear that in no case must the capital–output ratio exceed the level which corresponds to the point S.

On the lower part of Fig. 15 we now draw the curve $B''Z'$ representing $\Delta c/\Delta i$ for the curve BZ, i.e. the slope of its tangent for a given i. The curve $B''Z'$ will be situated below the horizontal line $B'N'$, as the slopes of all tangents to the curve BZ are less than the slope of the straight line BN. (The slope of a tangent at

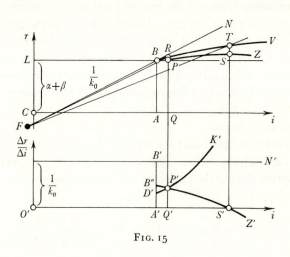

FIG. 15

any point of the curve BV must always be less than $1/k$ which, in turn, is less than $1/k_0$, i.e. than the slope of BN; the slope of a tangent to the curve BZ is in turn smaller than that of the tangent to the curve BV corresponding to the same i.) The curve $B''Y'$ obviously cuts the i-axis at the point S' corresponding to the point S.

Next we draw the 'decision curve' $D'K'$ which – according to the preceding chapter – is the same as that used in the case of an unlimited reserve of labour. The intersection of the two curves at point P' shows the rate of productive accumulation at the beginning of the period of 'recasting'; the projection of this point into the curve BV yields the rate of growth $r = OR$ at the beginning of this period; and its projection onto the curve BZ, the average rate of growth of consumption c. Finally, the slope of the straight line joining the point R on curve BV with point F yields the capital–output ratio which should be adopted.

The rate of productive accumulation and the rate of growth of consumption are much lower than in the case of a large reserve of labour. Indeed, in the latter case the rate of productive accumulation is determined by the point of intersection of the 'decision curve' and the horizontal line $B'N'$, and the rate of growth of consumption – on the assumption of a return after some long period to the initial rate of growth – by projecting this point onto the straight line BN.

4. If we disregard the question of the level of consumption *during* the period of 'recasting', the optimum solution is the case corresponding to the maximum S of the curve BZ – i.e. the capital–output ratio corresponding to the straight line FT. For in this way we obtain the highest possible average rate of growth of consumption over n years; this is tantamount to reaching the highest level of consumption which may be achieved given the supply of labour and the rate of growth $\alpha + \beta$ which will exist at the end of the period of 'recasting'. Many authors, especially in the West, concentrated their attention on this solution which was even nicknamed the 'golden rule'. However, it follows from our argument that this solution is purely theoretical in character because the key problem in the choice of capital intensity is the standard of living *in the course* of 'recasting'. The ascending 'decision curve' which allows for this factor leads, as we saw above, to the adoption of a much lower capital intensity and a lower average rate of growth of consumption during the period of 'recasting'.

It may be the case, at least theoretically, that in the initial position the capital intensity of aggregate productive capacity corresponds to a point on the curve BZ situated to the right of S; the curve BZ is thus downward sloping. The curve $B''Z'$ in the lower part of the diagram is then situated below the abscissa axis and obviously cannot intersect the curve of decision to the right of the initial position. This corresponds to the case, discussed above (section 1 of this chapter) of nonfulfilment of the criterion

$$(1+p)\frac{1-i_n}{1-i_0} > 1 \qquad (25)$$

In this case it is definitely advantageous to 'recast' aggregate equipment in order to *reduce* its capital intensity; this causes consumption to grow at a rate higher than r_0 in both the short and the long run.[†]

5. As in Chapter 4, section 3, we shall now discuss the problem of gradually achieving the increased rate of productive accumulation required at the beginning of the period of 'recasting'. Again we may imagine this is being done over transition period τ by using the gain from the normal increase in labour productivity resulting from technical progress (we denoted this rate of increase by α) exclusively for accumulation. This is the same assumption as we made when discussing the problem of accelerating growth by drawing on the reserve of labour.[‡]

It is clear that, as in the latter case, the transition period τ will be shorter, the higher the 'normal' rate of growth of labour productivity α resulting from technical progress.

6. It follows from the above that during the transition period the rate of growth of national income increases, but next declines over the n-year period of 'recasting', and at the end of this period the rate of growth falls back to its initial level. During the transition period τ the relative share of productive accumulation in the national income increases – i.e. this accumulation, and

[†] Cf. Kazimierz Łaski, 'Temporary slowing down of the growth and the dynamics of consumption in a socialist economy' (in Polish), *Ekonomista*, No. 4, 1964.

[‡] It should be noted, however, that there it meant the stabilization of real wages in the transition period, so that consumption grew *pari passu* with employment in this period. Here the situation is somewhat different. The acceleration of growth is based on a gradual increase in the capital intensity of investment and thus of labour productivity in new plant. As only the normal increase in labour productivity at a rate α is absorbed by productive accumulation, the additional increase in productivity serves to increase both consumption and accumulation in the same proportion. As a result, real wages do not remain stable throughout the transition period, but increase *pari passu* with the additional rise in productivity. This rise in real wages is in a way a counterpart to the rise in consumption during the transition period, which results from the acceleration of the increase in employment in the case of drawing on a reserve of labour.

particularly that of fixed capital, rises more rapidly than the national income. In the period of 'recasting' the process is reversed; the relative share of productive accumulation in the national income declines (although not to its initial level), so that productive accumulation increases less rapidly than the national income.

The question arises whether or not it would be possible to avoid the slackening of growth of national income in the period of 'recasting' and to maintain the rate reached at the end of the transition period. This is clearly impossible if the capital–output ratio, having been raised from k_0 to k in the transition period, remains thereafter at the same level, as has been assumed so far in our argument. For it follows from our preceding discussion that it is the rise in the capital–output ratio to a higher level that leads to an acceleration of growth, but that the *maintenance* of this ratio *at a constant level* thereafter is accompanied by a decline in the rate of growth back to the initial level.

From this it may in turn be concluded that it is possible to maintain the rate of growth of the national income at the level reached in the transition period if the capital–output ratio is increased steadily; the tendency of the rate of growth to decrease may then be counteracted by the effect of an adequate increase in the capital–output ratio on the productivity of labour. Obviously, the maintenance of a constant rate of growth of national income, based on a steadily rising capital–output ratio, will also call for a steady rise in the rate of productive accumulation.

Although it is possible in this way to keep the rate of growth at a constant level, it does not follow that such a policy is always sensible. It would clearly be unreasonable to continue such a process *ad infinitum*. Indeed, the steady increase in the rate of productive accumulation would ultimately bring the relative share of consumption in the national income down to zero, which would, of course, be absurd. Much earlier than that total consumption would begin to decrease, and *per capita* consumption earlier still. Thus it is clear that a policy of maintaining the rate of growth at a level higher than $r_0 = \alpha + \beta$ is conceivable only for a limited period. Sooner or later it must become necessary to put an end to the rise in the capital–output ratio, which will lead to a gradual slowing down in the growth of the national income, until it reaches the level r_0 as determined by the 'normal' growth of productivity of labour (resulting from technical progress) and the natural increase in the labour force.

If, however, there must sooner or later be a return to the rate of growth $\alpha + \beta$, this process must not be continued beyond the point of optimum capital intensity corresponding to the 'golden rule'. Moreover, there may be, and probably will be an even earlier decision to stabilize the capital intensity in order to achieve the gain in consumption sooner (cf. section 4 of this chapter).

7. So far we have been dealing with the problem of accelerating the growth of national income by raising the capital–output ratio on the assumption of neutral technical progress. We shall now consider the same problem for the case of technical progress 'encouraging capital intensity'.

In this case by adjusting aggregate productive capacity to a higher capital intensity we raise not only the average labour productivity but also the rate of its increase. For, after having completed the 'recasting' of aggregate capital equipment there is achieved not only a higher level of average productivity of labour (as in the case considered above), but also a higher future rate of increase in productivity than in the initial position – i.e. higher than α. Changes tending in this direction also occur throughout the course of 'recasting', because of the faster increase in productivity in the new plant. The effect of this is the greater, the more advanced the process of 'recasting'. At the beginning of the period of 'recasting' the influence of this factor is negligible. The fact that labour productivity in plant brought into operation in the first year exceeds that of the preceding year by α' (say, 5 per cent) rather than by α (say, 4 per cent) only slightly affects the growth of labour productivity in the economy as a whole; quantitatively much more important is the fact that the *level* of productivity in new plant is increased in the proportion

$1 + p$ after the start of 'recasting'. But at the end of the period of 'recasting' the rate of increase in *average* productivity is α' rather than α. The rising importance of the higher *rate of increase* in labour productivity in new plant neutralizes to some extent the tendency of growth due to the increased *level* of productivity of this plant to decline over the course of the period of 'recasting' (as described in our analysis of the case of neutral technical progress). The rate of increase in average productivity does not, therefore, decline to the initial level but to the level α' which is higher than α.

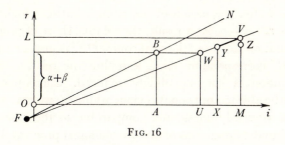

Fig. 16

The corresponding rate of growth of national income declines from the level r to the level $r_0 + \alpha' - \alpha$ which is higher than the initial rate r_0. This situation is represented in Fig. 16 which is similar to Fig. 14. In the present case the point depicting the rate of productive accumulation and the rate of growth of national income moves from V to Y rather than to W (as it did in the case of neutral technical progress) during the period of 'recasting'. But, as we shall see, the point W still retains some significance.

What benefits in the form of a faster long-run growth of consumption may be obtained in this case at the cost of raising the rate of productive accumulation at the beginning of the period of 'recasting' from i_0 to i (i.e. increasing i from OA to OM)?

In the case of neutral technical progress we defined this benefit as the increase in the average rate of growth of consumption over the period of 'recasting'. We indicated there the similarity between achieving the extra growth of consumption in this way over a period of 'recasting', and raising the rate of

73

growth of national income from r_0 to c by increasing the rate of productive accumulation by $i - i_0$ in the case of an unlimited reserve of labour (on the assumption that the rate of growth falls back to r_0 after n years); on this basis we applied the same 'decision curve' to the problem of the choice of capital intensity and the rate c as in the case of an unlimited reserve of labour. We would like to proceed in a similar fashion in the present case of technical progress 'encouraging capital intensity', but the following complication arises.

The rate of growth does not fall back to the initial level $r_0 = \alpha + \beta$ after the period of 'recasting', but to a higher level $\alpha' + \beta = r_0 + \alpha' - \alpha$. As a result, the relative share of productive accumulation in the national income, OX, is greater than the level OU corresponding to r_0, and thus the relative share of consumption is correspondingly reduced. Consequently, in order to be able to apply our previous argument we have to make the case presently considered comparable to the case of 're-casting' under conditions of neutral technical progress. For this purpose let us suppose that after the period of 'recasting' the rate of increase of the labour force is reduced to the level

$$\beta' = \beta + \alpha - \alpha'$$

by means of a steady reduction in hours worked. Then

$$\beta' + \alpha' = \beta + \alpha = r_0.$$

(Obviously this case is not quite equivalent to the return to the rate r_0 in the case of neutral technical progress because of the benefit of the gradual reduction in hours worked after the end of the period of 'recasting', but in view of the remoteness of the time when the benefit will accrue, the difference is not very important. The rate of productive accumulation will then drop to the level OU corresponding to r_0, and the relative share of consumption in the national income will rise *pro tanto*. We now have no difficulty in following our previous line of argument – i.e. we may relate the rate of growth of consumption c to the rate of productive accumulation at the beginning of the period of 'recasting' and apply the same 'decision curve' as in the case of an unlimited reserve of labour.

As above, let us denote the average rate of growth of national income over the period of 'recasting' by r_{av}. The average rate of increase in consumption (in the sense just discussed) is

$$c = (1 + r_{av})^n \bigg/ \sqrt{\left(\frac{1 - i_n}{1 - i_0}\right)} - 1$$

where i_n is the rate of accumulation which would obtain if the rate of growth returned to the level r_0 (in other words it is the abscissa of the point W). But is this not exactly the same result as in the case of neutral technical progress? The answer here is definitely negative; the rate of increase in productivity in new plant, α', which is higher than α, exerts its influence throughout the period of 'recasting' and thus neutralizes to some extent the tendency of the rate of growth of national income to decline. Consequently r_{av} is greater than in the previous case of neutral technical progress, where it was equal to

$$r_{av} = (1 + r_0) \sqrt[n]{(1 + p)} - 1$$

and as a result the average rate of growth of consumption is also greater. (The difference will, clearly, be more marked, the greater the difference $\alpha' - \alpha$.) This average rate of growth of consumption is represented in the diagram (Fig. 16) by the point Z, its abscissa being i and its ordinate c.

We may now construct a diagram similar to Fig. 15. Again we draw the curve BV for the rate of growth r at the beginning of the period of 'recasting'; this curve is the locus of the point V in Fig. 16. The curve BY which represents the rate of growth at the end of the period (i.e. $r_0 + \alpha' - \alpha$) is the locus of the point Y. The latter curve is upward sloping since, according to our definition of technical progress 'encouraging capital intensity', the rate of increase in productivity α' is greater, the higher the capital–output ratio k. Finally, the curve BZ represents the average rate of growth of consumption c (on the assumption that, after the end of the period of 'recasting' the current rate of growth

75

$r_0 + \alpha' - \alpha$ will be reduced to r_0). This curve is the locus of the point Z and, as follows from our argument, it is situated above the curve BZ of Fig. 15 corresponding to the case of neutral technical progress. For this very reason the rate of productive accumulation i, determined in Fig. 17 by the point of intersection P' of the 'decision curve' and the curve $\Delta c/\Delta i$, is higher than in the case of neutral technical progress, and so is the average rate

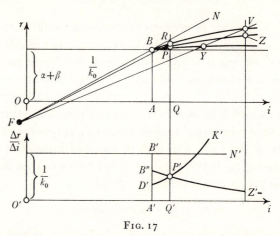

FIG. 17

of growth of consumption c. Obviously, the capital–output ratio k (being the reciprocal of the slope of the straight line FR) is also greater than it was in that case. This means that in our present case a higher capital–output ratio will be chosen, because *ceteris paribus* we obtain a greater increase in consumption. This is to be expected, as we are dealing here with technical progress 'encouraging capital intensity'.†

† In the case of technical progress 'encouraging capital intensity' it is impossible to show, as in section 6, that the curve of the average rate of growth of consumption BZ has a peak, because this rate tends to increase along with α' which in turn is an increasing function of capital intensity (see preceding page). Thus the problem of the 'golden rule' does not arise in this case.

9. INCREASING THE RATE OF GROWTH OF NATIONAL INCOME UNDER CONDITIONS OF FULL EMPLOYMENT THROUGH A REDUCTION IN THE LIFE-SPAN OF EQUIPMENT

1. We shall consider now the problem of accelerating the growth of the national income by increasing the average productivity of labour through a reduction in the life-span of equipment from n to n' years. As a result of a shorter life-span of equipment average productivity is raised to a higher level because aggregate fixed capital is, on the average, made 'younger' and thus techniques of production are more up-to-date. The process of 'rejuvenating' the stock of capital equipment is achieved by intensifying the scrapping of existing productive capacity in the proportion a/a_0 where a_0 is the parameter of depreciation corresponding to a life-span of n years and a constant rate of growth r_0, whilst a is the parameter corresponding to the same rate of growth and a life-span of n' years (see Chapter 7, section 5). During the period of 'rejuvenation' which lasts n' years, there is an additional increase in the productivity of labour in the proportion $1 + p$. As in the case of neutral technical progress, the increase in the rate of growth of national income, $r - r_0$, equal to the increase in the rate of growth of average productivity, is highest at the beginning of the period of 'rejuvenation' and declines gradually throughout the process, since the extra scrapping applies to less and less obsolete plant. Finally $r - r_0$ reaches zero, when the process of 'rejuvenation' is complete.†

† As shown in note, ‡, p. 60, the system is then poised for uniform growth at a rate r_0.

But the rate of productive accumulation i_n is higher than in the initial situation – i.e. than i_0 – since the reduced life-span of fixed capital involves higher investment.

The necessary precondition for such an operation to be worth carrying out is again

$$(1+p)\frac{1-i_{n'}}{1-i_0} > 1 \tag{26}$$

which means that it brings about an additional increase in consumption. The difference between the present case and that of 'recasting' of the stock of capital with neutral technical progress is that the rate of productive accumulation is raised from i_0 to $i_{n'}$ not because of the increased capital–output ratio k, but as a result of the rise in the parameter of depreciation a which represents the rate of contraction of the national income caused by scrapping old plant. The inequality given above may be rewritten in the form

$$(1+p)\left(1-\frac{i_{n'}-i_0}{1-i_0}\right) > 1$$

We may determine $i_{n'}-i_0$ from our equations for r_0 at the beginning and at the end of the period of rejuvenation

$$r_0 = \frac{1}{k}i_0 - \frac{m}{k}(a_0-u)$$

$$r_0 = \frac{1}{k}i_{n'} - \frac{m}{k}(a-u)$$

From this we derive

$$i_{n'}-i_0 = m(a-a_0)$$

Thus our precondition for the 'rejuvenation' of the aggregate fixed capital to be worth carrying out may be written in the form

$$(1+p)\left(1-\frac{m(a-a_0)}{1-i_0}\right) > 1 \tag{27}$$

The process of 'rejuvenation' can be represented diagrammatically analogously to Fig. 14. The parameter of depreciation increases from a_0 to a (which is reflected in a parallel downward shift of the line CN).† At the beginning of the period of 're-juvenation' we obtain a higher rate of growth of national income r with a considerably increased rate of productive accumulation i (see Fig. 18). During the period of 'rejuvenation', the point representing the rate of accumulation and the rate of growth of

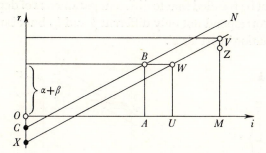

Fig. 18

the national income moves gradually from V to W.‡ As a result, the rate of growth is brought back to its initial level r_0, with a higher rate of productive accumulation. The diagram also shows the point Z whose ordinate c, the average rate of growth of

† This is strictly true only at the beginning and end of the 'rejuvenation' process (cf. note †, p. 63).

‡ It should be noted that the presentation of the process of 'rejuvenation' in Fig. 18 is not quite accurate. The point X is not in fact fully immobile in the course of this process. Indeed, the productive capacities P_1, P_2, etc. existing in the initial position (cf. note ‡, p. 60) form a geometrical progression with a quotient

$$(1+r_0)/(1+u).$$

The same is true of capacities scrapped, i.e. of

$$\frac{a}{a_0} P_1, \quad \frac{a}{a_0} P_2, \quad \dots$$

The corresponding actual losses of output will also form a geometrical progression but its quotient will be

$$\frac{1+r_0}{1+u} \cdot (1+u) = 1+r_0$$

because of the operation of the factor u. However, in the course of the process of 'rejuvenation' the rate of growth of the national income is higher than r_0. As a result the point X moves upwards and the straight line XV also shifts upwards, but without changing its slope. At the end of the period of 'rejuvenation' there will be a return to the position XV shown in Fig. 18.

consumption, is determined by the formula

$$(1+r_0)^{n'} \bigg/ \sqrt{\left((1+p)\frac{1-i_{n'}}{1-i_0}\right)} - 1$$

while its abscissa is the rate of productive accumulation at the
beginning of the period of 'rejuvenation' (see Fig. 18).

It must be recalled that to different parameters of depreciation
a there correspond not only different p and $i_{n'}$ but also different
'rejuvenation' periods n'.

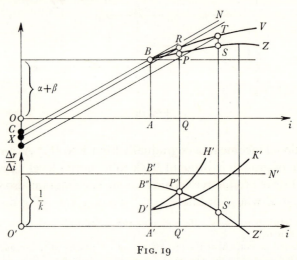

FIG. 19

2. We may now construct a diagram similar to Fig. 15 which
showed the choice of the capital–output ratio in the case of
neutral technical progress. In the upper part of the diagram
(see Fig. 19) we draw the curves of the rate of growth of the
national income at the beginning of the period of rejuvenation r
and of the average rate of growth of consumption c. Since this
average is calculated for different periods n' (n' is shorter, the
higher is a) we must modify the 'decision curve' as was done in
the case of a limited reserve of labour. For the further we move to
the right, the shorter becomes the period during which consumption grows at the average rate c, and this rate must therefore be
appreciated less (see Chapter 5, section 2). Accordingly, the

'decision curve' $D'K'$ is replaced by another 'decision curve' $D'H'$. The point of intersection of the curves $D'H'$ and $B''Z'$ again determines i, c and r. Drawing a parallel to the line CN through the point R we obtain the increase in the parameter of depreciation $a - a_0$ (equal to the distance CX divided by m/k).

3. According to formula (27) the additional increase in consumption from the initial position to the end of the process of 'rejuvenation' is equal to

$$(1 + p)\frac{1 - i_{n'}}{1 - i_0} = (1 + p)\left[1 - \frac{m(a - a_0)}{1 - i_0}\right]$$

It is clear that this expression – which in the case of a rational reduction of the life-span of equipment is greater than one – has a maximum for a certain n'. Indeed, if the intended life-span of equipment n' is already very short, so that average productivity in the economy is very close to that in the new plant, a further considerable relative reduction in n' raises p only negligibly although the parameter of depreciation a shows a significant increase. This means that the first factor of the expression on the right-hand side increases very little while the second one declines considerably.

Thus there arises here a situation similar to that in the case of 'recasting' under conditions of neutral technical progress discussed above where the increase in consumption reaches a maximum for a certain capital intensity according to the expression

$$(1 + p)\frac{1 - i_n}{1 - i_0} = (1 + p)\left[1 - \frac{(r_0 + a - u)(k - k_0)}{1 - i_0}\right] \qquad (23')$$

But in contrast to that case, the maximum 'once-for-all' increase in consumption attainable in the present case of 'rejuvenation' of fixed capital *does not* correspond to the highest point on the curve BZ. The average rate of growth of consumption during the period of 'rejuvenation' given by BZ increases towards a maximum as n' falls for two reasons: (1) because of the increase in the expression

$$(1 + p)\left[1 - \frac{m(a - a_0)}{1 - i_0}\right]$$

and (2) because of the reduction in the length of the 'rejuvenation' period which is equal to n'. As a result the highest point on the curve BZ will be reached at a point of more intensive 'rejuvenation' – i.e. at a higher a – than that corresponding to the maximum absolute increase in consumption; this means that the highest attainable level of consumption after the period of 'rejuvenation' corresponds to a point S situated to the left of the peak of the curve BZ (see Fig. 19).

However – as in the case of 'recasting' fixed capital with neutral technical progress – the degree of 'rejuvenation' of aggregate capital equipment chosen by the government according to Fig. 19 will be lower than that which assures the maximum level of consumption after the process of 'rejuvenation' (and obviously this will be even more the case with regard to the degree of 'rejuvenation' which produces the highest average rate of growth of national income over the period of 'rejuvenation').

4. We considered above the process of 'recasting' to obtain a higher capital intensity of aggregate productive capacity with a given life-span of equipment and the process of 'rejuvenation' of fixed capital with a given capital intensity. A more general procedure for accelerating the growth of national income would be a combination of the two processes. Such a 'transformation' of fixed capital would consist of a simultaneous raising of the capital intensity from m_0 to m, and of the parameter of depreciation from a_0 (corresponding to a life-span of equipment n) to a (corresponding to a life-span of equipment n'). As this essay deals merely with basic and relatively simple elements in the theory of growth for a socialist economy, we shall confine ourselves here to the problem of the optimum capital intensity (assuming neutral technical progress) and life-span of equipment without allowing for 'sacrifices' of consumption *in the course* of the 'transformation' process. This is a generalization of the problems considered above, of the optimum capital intensity of equipment with a given life-span, and vice versa (Chapter 8, section 4 and the preceding section of this chapter).

Increasing growth by reduction in life-span of equipment

In the initial position we have

$$r_0 = \alpha + \beta = \frac{i_0}{k_0} - \frac{m_0}{k_0}(a_0 - u) \tag{28}$$

Let us denote the rate of productive accumulation in the optimum position by i' and the proportional increase in the average labour productivity resulting from raising the capital intensity and reducing the life-span of equipment by $1 + p$. According to section 1 of Chapter 8 and section 1 of this chapter the proportional extra increase in consumption during the 'transformation' period will be

$$(1 + p)\frac{1 - i'}{1 - i_0} = (1 + p)\left(1 - \frac{i' - i}{1 - i_0}\right)$$

After the period of 'transformation' (assuming neutral technical progress) we have

$$r_0 = \alpha + \beta = \frac{i'}{k} - \frac{m}{k}(a - u) \tag{29}$$

where $k - k_0 = m - m_0 > 0$ as a result of raising the capital–output ratio, and $a - a_0 > 0$ as a result of reducing the life-span of equipment. From equations (28) and (29) we obtain

$$(k - k_0)r_0 = i' - i_0 - (ma - m_0 a_0) + (m - m_0)u$$

and taking into consideration that $k - k_0 = m - m_0$

$$i' - i_0 = (m - m_0)(r_0 - u) + (ma - m_0 a) + (m_0 a - m_0 a_0)$$

$$= (m - m_0)(r_0 - u + a) + m_0(a - a_0)$$

Hence the extra proportional increase in consumption is

$$(1 + p)\left[1 - \frac{(m - m_0)(r_0 - u + a) + m_0(a - a_0)}{1 - i_0}\right]$$

Now, the higher are $m - m_0$ and $a - a_0$, the greater is $1 + p$, but the smaller the second factor. The point at which the product reaches its maximum – and it follows from the argument in section 4 of Chapter 8 and in section 3 of this chapter that there does exist a combination of m and a for which this occurs – is an

6-2

A socialist economy

optimum solution both with regard to the capital intensity and the life-span of equipment. In this position a given labour force increasing at a rate β, with productivity increasing at a rate α as a result of technical progress, will secure the highest possible consumption increasing at a rate $\alpha + \beta$. This will therefore give the highest possible real wage increasing at a rate α.

As implied above in the consideration of an optimum m for a given n and vice versa the achievement of this 'paradise' may, however, prove to be too costly from the point of view of consumption in the short run, during the 'transformation' of fixed capital.

It should still be borne in mind that to achieve a complete presentation of the problems of 'recasting' and 'rejuvenation' of fixed capital, the problem of foreign trade difficulties should be superimposed on these processes. These difficulties naturally restrain the government's tendency to accelerate the growth of national income in this way; but, as we have repeatedly stated, this essay deals merely with the basic elements in the theory of growth for a socialist economy, and we shall not embark here upon a detailed discussion of this subject.

10. THE PROBLEM OF CHOICE OF THE CAPITAL–OUTPUT RATIO UNDER CONDITIONS OF AN UNLIMITED SUPPLY OF LABOUR

1. In the two preceding chapters we dealt with the problem of accelerating the growth of national income under conditions of full employment. It was shown that, at least for the period of 'recasting', such an acceleration may be achieved by raising the capital–output ratio so as to increase labour productivity in new plant. In the case of an unlimited supply of labour the rate of national income can be increased without changing the capital–output ratio by accelerating the increase in employment. It was on this assumption that we based our discussion in Chapter 4. However, from the fact that it is possible in this way to increase the rate of growth of national income over and above the level $r_0 = \alpha + \beta$ (i.e. that determined by the increase in productivity resulting from technical progress and the natural increase in the labour force), it does not necessarily follow that this is the best method to choose.

It is easy to envisage here the possibility of reducing the capital–output ratio by fuller utilization of existing labour resources (if these possibilities have not already been exhausted). We shall examine this problem in detail below, but first we shall deal with the views of Dobb and Sen on the subject. These authors drew attention to the fact that, on certain assumptions, it may be reasonable to *raise* the capital–output ratio even in the case of an unlimited supply of labour.† Their argument, adapted to the approach used in this book, may be presented as follows.

Suppose that the government aims at the fastest possible rate

† M. Dobb, *An essay on Economic Growth and Planning*, Routledge and Kegan Paul, London, 1960; A. K. Sen, *Choice of Techniques*, Basil Blackwell, Oxford, 1960.

of economic development without resorting to a reduction in real wages. It thus decides to maintain these wages at a constant level for a long period, while using the whole increase in labour productivity to raise the rate of accumulation. We discussed above (see Chapter 4, section 5) such an increase in the rate of accumulation based upon the rise in labour productivity resulting from technical progress during the 'transition period' τ. But it is also possible for this increase in the share of productive accumulation in the national income to be reinforced by 'recasting' the stock of equipment in order to raise its capital intensity; this would result in an additional increase in productivity in the relevant period. When the capital–output ratio is maintained at its initial level k_0 the increase in the national income relative to consumption after n years is raised in the proportion $(1+\alpha)^n$ (cf. Chapter 4, section 5).† But if we superimpose upon this the process of 'recasting' which brings the capital–intensity up to the level k, the national income will be increased in relation to consumption in the proportion $(1+\alpha)^n(1+p)$, where p is the proportional increase in productivity in the new plant resulting from raising the capital–output ratio from k_0 to k.‡ Let us denote by i_0 the rate of productive accumulation in the initial position; by π_n the rate of accumulation n years later with the capital–output ratio remaining unchanged at the level k_0; and by π_n' the rate of accumulation n years later, but on the assumption that the stock of equipment has been 'recast' in order to raise its capital intensity to k. We then have

$$i_0 < \pi_n < \pi_n'$$

The respective rates of growth of national income will be as follows:

$$r_0 = \frac{1}{k_0} i_0 - \frac{m_0}{k_0}(a-u)$$

† In fact average productivity increases in a proportion somewhat higher than $(1+\alpha)^n$ because the acceleration of growth of the national income causes some decline in the average 'age' of equipment. We shall get round this complication by using this slight increase in average productivity to raise real wages somewhat.

‡ Cf. note † above.

86

Choice of capital–output ratio

$$r_n = \frac{1}{k_0} \pi_n - \frac{m_0}{k_0} (a_n - u)$$

$$r'_n = \frac{1}{k} \pi'_n - \frac{m}{k} (a'_n - u)$$

It is clear that $r_n > r_0$, but it cannot be taken for granted that $r'_n > r_n$. It is true that the rate of accumulation π'_n is higher than π_n, but on the other hand, $k > k_0$ which adversely affects the rate of growth. If we disregard the relatively small difference between the terms

$$\frac{m_0}{k_0} (a_n - u) \quad \text{and} \quad \frac{m}{k} (a'_n - u)$$

we obtain the following condition for r'_n to be greater than r_n:

$$\frac{\pi'_n}{k} > \frac{\pi_n}{k_0}$$

In other words, the necessary condition for achieving a higher rate of growth as a result of adjusting fixed capital to a higher capital intensity is a greater relative increase in the rate of accumulation than in capital intensity. Even if such is the case, however, it is not by itself a conclusive argument for raising the capital–output ratio; in addition we must take into account (as we do throughout this essay) not only what happens in the long run – i.e., in this case, at the end of the n-year period of 'recasting' – but also what will occur in the near future. Now, the rate of growth at the *beginning* of the period of 'recasting' is

$$r'_0 = \frac{1}{k} i_0 - \frac{m}{k} (a - u)$$

since the rise in the productivity of labour (resulting either from technical progress or from raising the capital–output ratio) is not yet able to affect the rate of accumulation. It is clear that the rate of growth due to the rise in the capital–output ratio, r'_0, is lower than $r_0 = \alpha + \beta$. Consequently in this period an increase in unemployment will occur, the rate of growth of the national income being lower than the rate of increase in labour productivity plus the natural rate of growth of the labour force. Thus it is not at all certain that the government will decide to raise the capital–output ratio, even if this would bring about a substantial increase in the rate of growth at later stages of the process of 'recasting'. Moreover, we shall try to show that the idea of raising the capital–output ratio, given a reserve of labour, would probably yield no benefits even in the long run unless the rate of increase in labour productivity resulting from technical progress, α, is very small. As a matter of fact neither Dobb nor Sen took this type of increase in productivity into consideration at all; they assumed the rise in productivity to be achieved solely by raising the capital–output ratio.

In order to examine the problem of an optimum capital–output ratio under conditions of unlimited labour supply we shall again use a diagrammatic presentation. We shall begin with the case discussed by Dobb and Sen when $\alpha = 0$.

2. The ratio of national income to consumption is $1/(1-i)$, since i being the rate of productive accumulation, the relative share of consumption in the national income is $1-i$. Hence, initially this ratio is equal to $1/(1-i_0)$, while at the end of the period of 'recasting' it equals $1/(1-\pi_n')$. Since for the time being we disregard technical progress, so that $\alpha = 0$, the national income per worker will increase over the period of 'recasting' in the proportion $1+p$. Since real wages are kept constant, the ratio of the national income to consumption will also increase in the proportion $1+p$. Thus we have

$$\frac{\dfrac{1}{1-\pi_n'}}{\dfrac{1}{1-i_0}} = 1-p$$

or

$$1-\pi_n' = \frac{1-i_0}{1+p}$$

and

$$\pi_n' = 1 - \frac{1-i_0}{1+p} \tag{30}$$

We now plot k as the abscissa and

$$\frac{1-i_0}{1+p}$$

as the ordinate (see Fig. 20). To the abscissa $k_0 = OD$ there corresponds the ordinate $1 - i_0 = BD$, as in this case the capital–output ratio has not been raised and $p = 0$. It is clear that the curve BT is simply a production curve like that in Fig. 11, p. 53, except that it is shifted to the right and the scale of the ordinate

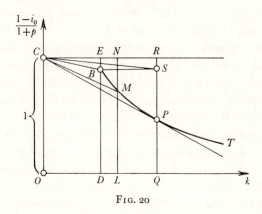

Fig. 20

axis is different. Indeed, employment per unit increment in national income is proportional to the reciprocal of $1 + p$ which is the index of labour productivity in new plant. Moreover, k is the sum of $m + \mu$ where m is the capital–output ratio for investment in fixed capital and μ the corresponding ratio for the increase in inventories. When m increases μ remains unaltered, so that the production curve in Fig. 20 is shifted to the right by a distance μ as compared with that in Fig. 11 (i.e. m in Fig. 11 corresponds to $m + \mu$ in Fig. 20).

It follows from formula (30) that for a given k the rate π'_n is equal to the distance MN between the curve BT and the horizontal line CN drawn at a distance equal to 1 from the k-axis. Hence the slope of the segment CM equals π'_n/k, since

$$MN = \pi'_n \quad \text{and} \quad OL = CN = k.$$

As shown above, the ratio π'_n/k determines the rate of growth at the end of the period of 'recasting'.

It is now easy to answer the question how far the capital–output ratio should be raised in order to maximize the rate of growth at the end of the period of 'recasting' in the case represented by Fig. 20. The slope of the straight line joining the point C with any point on the curve BT is greatest at the point P – i.e. when the straight line is a tangent to the curve BT. Hence the capital–output ratio should be raised to the level shown by the abscissa of point P – i.e. OQ – but not beyond this point.†

This is not, however, the end of the problem as we must also see what happens in the early stages of 'recasting'. If the capital–output ratio were not raised at all, the rate of growth would be determined by the ratio i_0/k_0 which is represented in the diagram by the slope of the straight line CB. (It must be recalled that $BD = 1 - i_0$, so that $EB = 1 - (1 - i_0) = i_0$, while $OD = CE = k_0$.) However, when the capital–output ratio is raised to the level $k = OQ = CR$, then at the beginning of the period of 'recasting' instead of i_0/k_0 we have the ratio i_0/k which is represented by the slope of the straight line CS. Thus we gain a higher rate of growth in the long run (this is shown by the difference between the slopes of the straight lines CP and CB), but we lose in terms of the near future (as shown by the difference between the slopes of the straight lines CB and CS).

In this case the government would probably choose a capital–output ratio somewhere between the levels $k_0 = OD$ and $k = OQ$, or might decide after all to maintain the level k_0.

3. We shall now take into account the increase in the productivity of labour resulting from technical progress, confining ourselves to the case where this progress is neutral; we shall see that the situation is radically changed even when the rate of growth of productivity is rather slight. The ratio of national income to consumption will then increase over n years in the

† The rate of growth equal to the slope of CP is closely akin to that yielded by J. von Neumann's model because it is the highest rate of growth under conditions of an unlimited supply of labour with a given constant real wage.

proportion $(1+\alpha)^n (1+p)$, real wages remaining constant.†
(Since we assumed neutral technical progress, the rate of growth
of productivity α, does not depend upon the capital–output ratio.)
Thus we now have:

$$\frac{\dfrac{1}{1-\pi'_n}}{\dfrac{1}{1-i_0}} = (1+\alpha)^n (1+p)$$

or

$$1 - \pi'_n = \frac{1-i_0}{1+p} \cdot \frac{1}{(1+\alpha)^n}$$

and thus

$$\pi'_n = 1 - \frac{1-i_0}{1+p} \cdot \frac{1}{(1+\alpha)^n} \qquad (31)$$

If we do not raise the capital–output ratio above the level k_0, then
$p = 0$ and the rate of growth after n years obtained from formula
(31) results from the increase in productivity which is due solely
to technical progress, real wages remaining constant:

$$\pi_n = 1 - (1-i_0)\frac{1}{(1+\alpha)^n}$$

We shall now represent diagrammatically the relationship
between

$$\frac{1-i_0}{1+p} \cdot \frac{1}{(1+\alpha)^n}$$

and k, analogously to Fig. 20. We begin by drawing the curve

$$\frac{1-i_0}{1+p}$$

(identical to BT in Fig. 20). We then divide its ordinates by
$(1+\alpha)^n$ and thus obtain the curve $B'T'$. (We assumed here that
α took the relatively low level of 2.5 per cent and that $n = 20$
years; hence $(1+\alpha)^n$ is equal to 1.65 and it is this figure that was
used to deflate the ordinates of the curve BT in the diagram.)
For any given k the rate π'_n is now equal to the distance NM'
between the curve $B'T'$ and the horizontal line CN which is

† Or rather, increasing somewhat; cf. note †, p. 86.

drawn at a unit distance from the k-axis. To $k_0 = OD$, there corresponds

$$\pi_n = B'E = 1 - (1 - i_0)\frac{1}{(1 + \alpha)^n}$$

since in this case $p = 0$.

The slope of the straight line CM' which joins the point C with the point M' on the curve $B'T'$ represents the ratio π_n'/k. In particular it should be noted that the slope of the straight line CB' is equal to π_n/k_0. Finally, the slopes of the straight lines CB and CK represent the ratios i_0/k_0 and i_0/k respectively (cf. Fig. 20). It is clear that in the case represented in Fig. 21 it is not desirable

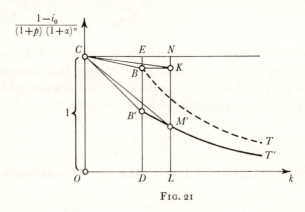

Fig. 21

to raise the capital–output ratio above the level k_0. Indeed, when the point M' moves to the right along the curve $B'T'$ the slope of the straight line CM' diminishes; this means that $\pi_n'/k < \pi_n/k_0$ so that raising the capital–output ratio leads to a decrease in the rate of growth of national income at the end of the period of 'recasting'. Obviously the same is true of the rate at the beginning of this period (the slope of the straight line CN is smaller than that of the straight line CB).

Thus it may be seen that, while in the case of $\alpha = 0$ (as depicted by Fig. 20) the rate of growth at the end of the period of 'recasting' is at a maximum for a capital–output ratio about twice as high as that in the initial situation – with a moderate increase in productivity ($\alpha = 2.5$ per cent p.a.) resulting from technical progress, this rate of growth is adversely affected by a rise in the capital–output ratio. Thus technical progress, as reflected in the downward shift of the curve of production, considerably reduces the practical significance of the Dobb–Sen approach.

4. We have so far assumed that real wages remain unaltered for a very long period so that consumption rises only as a result of increasing employment. Such an assumption is not very realistic. When considering economic growth with a reserve of labour in Chapter 4 we assumed that real wages remained constant only for a rather short transition period which made it possible – with labour productivity increasing at a rate α owing to technical progress – to produce a definite increase in the rate of accumulation (see section 5 of that chapter). The transition period being over, real wages once again begin to rise at a rate α accompanied by a more rapid increase in employment than was the case in the initial position. One might proceed in a somewhat different fashion by permitting real wages to increase over a long period at a rate lower than the rate of growth of productivity α. As a result, by the end of n years the ratio of national income to consumption would have been increased in the proportion $(1 + \alpha - \sigma)^z$ where σ is, of course, less than α.

It is clear that if this line is followed the Dobb–Sen approach recovers its significance to some extent. When the capital–output ratio is raised from k_0 to k, national income increases relative to consumption in the proportion $(1 + \alpha - \sigma)^n(1 + p)$. Equation (31) now takes the form:

$$\frac{\dfrac{1}{1 - \pi'_n}}{\dfrac{1}{1 - i_0}} = (1 + p)(1 + \alpha - \sigma)^n$$

or

$$\pi'_n = 1 - \frac{1 - i_0}{1 + p} \frac{1}{(1 + \alpha - \sigma)^n} \tag{32}$$

This result differs from formula (31) in that we now have $(1 + \alpha - \sigma)^n$ rather than $(1 + \alpha)^n$ in the denominator of the last term on the right-hand side of the equation. The present case is equivalent to the case examined above in which the rate of growth of productivity resulting from technical progress would be assumed $\alpha - \sigma$ rather than α. And it followed from the above that the lower the rate of growth of productivity α, the greater was the chance that raising the capital–output ratio with the reserve of labour in existence would prove a profitable proposition.

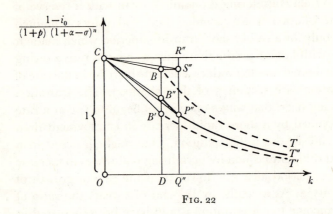

FIG. 22

In Fig. 22 we draw the curve

$$\frac{1 - i_0}{(1 + p)(1 + \alpha - \sigma)^n}$$

along with the curves

$$\frac{1 - i_0}{1 + p} \quad \text{and} \quad \frac{1 - i_0}{(1 + p)(1 + \alpha \quad ^n}$$

reproduced from Fig. 21. We assume that $\sigma = 1$ per cent, so that α having previously been fixed at 2.5 per cent, we now have $\alpha - \sigma = 1.5$ per cent. It will be seen that, even with $\alpha - \sigma$ as low as this, the Dobb–Sen approach is of little significance. The diagram shows that the optimum solution – i.e. the slope of the straight line OP'' – does not differ much from π_n, i.e. from the slope of the straight line CB''.

94

Our analysis seems to lead ultimately to the conclusion that the theory that economic growth should be accelerated by increasing the capital–output ratio has probably no major practical significance in the case where there exists a reserve of labour; however, the fact that the theory demonstrated a new aspect of the problem of choice of production techniques considerably increased the scope of the discussion of this subject.

5. In the above discussion we expressed some doubts as to the advisability of 'recasting' the stock of equipment in order to raise its capital intensity, given an unlimited reserve of labour (and neutral technical progress). However, we should still examine whether it is not advisable under such conditions to *reduce* the capital intensity of the stock of equipment. In this discussion we shall maintain Dobb and Sen's rule that real wages must not decline at any phase of the process involved. This already imposes some limitations upon the application of less capital- and more labour-intensive methods of production. But even more basic is the question of the physical possibility of reducing capital intensity in underdeveloped countries. Indeed, it should be kept in mind that in any branch of industry there is some minimum capital–output ratio which may be fairly high. Application of more primitive techniques may not be capable of reducing the capital intensity of production. It is difficult even to imagine primitive variants, for example, with regard to chemical processes. But even where such variants do exist they are not always less capital-intensive. It appears, for instance, that the spinning wheel is more capital-intensive than modern spinning machinery. On the other hand there do exist industries even in underdeveloped countries where it is possible to reduce the capital–output ratio by choosing methods which involve less investment and more labour, e.g. cotton weaving, building, transport.

6. For the analysis of the influence of a reduction in m we shall use a diagram similar to Fig. 14. (For the present we shall ignore foreign trade difficulties; these will be dealt with at a later stage.) As in that case we denote the capital–output ratio (in

95

relation to fixed capital and inventories) in the initial position by k_0. But instead of discussing increasing the capital–output ratio we assume that it is possible to reduce it to some extent and hence that $k < k_0$. Thus to the same rate of productive accumulation there now corresponds a higher r (see Fig. 23).

In particular, to $i_0 = OA$ – the rate of productive accumulation which corresponded in the initial position to $\alpha + \beta$ – there now corresponds the rate of growth $AE = \alpha + \beta + \gamma$. The increase in

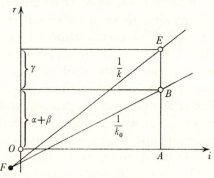

Fig. 23

employment is based to the extent β on the natural increase in the labour force and to the extent γ on drawing on the labour reserve. $\beta + \gamma$ is not, however, the total rate of expansion of employment. The initial rate of increase in productivity resulting from technical progress is α. It is obvious that after the reduction of the capital–output ratio from k_0 to k this rate cannot be maintained, since new equipment will be of a lower capital intensity than existing equipment with the capital–output ratio k_0, and will therefore also be characterized by correspondingly lower labour productivity. It follows that the annual rate of increase in productivity will be less than the rate α resulting from technical progress. However, as time goes by the situation will change. As the stock of equipment is gradually saturated with less capital-intensive techniques characterized by lower productivity, the rate of increase of average productivity will diverge less and less from α.

Choice of capital–output ratio

Finally when all the equipment is endowed with the new less capital-intensive technique, because all old equipment has been scrapped, the rate of increase in productivity will return to the level α.[†] (It is clear that this process is in a sense symmetrical with 'recasting' the stock of equipment with the aim of raising its capital intensity.)

The changes in national income, productivity, and equipment outlined above are illustrated by Fig. 24.

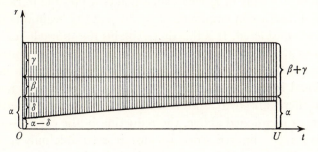

FIG. 24

The ordinate is the rate of growth r, and the abscissa time t. The diagram shows how productivity and employment change in the course of 'recasting' which aims at a lower capital intensity. At the beginning of the process the rate of growth of average productivity is $\alpha - \delta$ where δ represents the effect of the first batch of equipment to be characterized by a lower capital intensity and a lower productivity of labour than the old equipment. This is compensated by an increase of δ in the rate of expansion of employment, in addition to β (the natural increase in the labour force) and γ (drawing on the labour reserve to increase the rate of growth of national income to $\alpha + \beta + \gamma$). Thus the total rate of growth of employment is $\beta + \delta + \gamma$, of which $\delta + \gamma$ depends on drawing on the labour reserve. As time goes by the deviation of the rate of increase in productivity from α declines, and after all the equipment has been endowed with a lower capital intensity

† As already mentioned, throughout this chapter we assume neutral technical progress.

and lower labour productivity this rate will go back to the level α. Thus the rate of increase in productivity rises from $\alpha - \delta$ at the beginning of the period to α at its end; conversely the rate of increase in employment declines from $\beta + \gamma + \delta$ to $\beta + \gamma$ (shaded area).

It is obvious that the acceleration of growth from $\alpha + \beta$ to $\alpha + \beta + \gamma$ without increasing the relative share of productive accumulation in the national income is feasible because of the unlimited supply of labour which makes it possible to raise the rate of increase in employment by $\delta + \gamma$ at the beginning of the period considered. It is this that explains the 'miracle' of being able to accelerate the growth of national income *and* consumption (the relative share of productive accumulation in the national income remaining unchanged). It should be noticed that there are two limitations to this rewarding operation. First, as mentioned above, the reduction in the capital–output ratio k has a limited scope because it is feasible only in some industries. Second, the reduction in k should not be pushed so far as to make δ higher than α and thus $\alpha - \delta$ negative, since that would mean an *absolute decline* in labour productivity. This, however, would cause a fall in real wages which would violate the condition we set: indeed, consumption would increase *pari passu* with national income at a rate $\alpha + \beta + \gamma$, and employment at a higher rate, $\delta + \beta + \gamma$. (If $\delta < \alpha$ real wages would be growing but at a rate lower than α p.a.)

7. It is still interesting to consider what happens at the end of the period OU if drawing upon the labour reserve in the course of that period has led to its exhaustion. In this case the rate of growth cannot be maintained at the level $\alpha + \beta + \gamma$ in the subsequent period and has to drop to $\alpha + \beta$, because no further drawing on the labour reserve is possible. If a higher rate of growth than this is desired, then it is necessary to reverse the process described by raising the capital–output ratio. This may appear paradoxical because having adjusted the equipment to a lower capital intensity, we now try to go back to our starting point. However, in the meantime surplus labour has been

absorbed and national income and consumption increased at a high rate. Having achieved full employment we may either go back to the initial rate of growth or, if we desire a higher rate, we have to reverse the process and 'recast' equipment in order to increase its capital intensity because we no longer have the advantage of a labour reserve from which we benefited in the past.

The more capital intensive technique is not *per se* either superior or inferior: the choice of the 'right' capital intensity

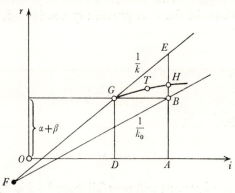

FIG. 25

depends on the availability of labour (allowing, as mentioned above, for technological limitations and maintenance of real wages).

8. Let us now take foreign trade difficulties into consideration. We shall again use a diagrammatic presentation (see Fig. 25).

Imagine that after a reduction in the capital–output ratio from k_0 to k we then leave the rate of growth unchanged at $\alpha + \beta$. The relative share of productive accumulation in the national income would then decline to OD. Now if instead we had chosen to increase the rate of growth above that level this would have involved difficulties with foreign trade. As a result the relation between i and r is represented in Fig. 25 by the curve GH rather than by the straight line FE (cf. Fig. 6). If the curve GH is rather flat (as on the chart) the gain in the rate of growth will be small.

7-2

In such a case it may be reasonable to leave the rate of growth at the level $\alpha + \beta$ rather than to increase it – thus gaining the advantage of a smaller relative share of productive accumulation in the national income. In this case by reducing the capital–output ratio from k_0 to k a higher relative share of consumption in the national income is achieved without impairing the rate of growth. This results in an immediate increase in the level of consumption without reducing its future rate of increase below $\alpha + \beta$. The changes in the rate of increase in productivity will be similar to those in the case previously considered. The rate of

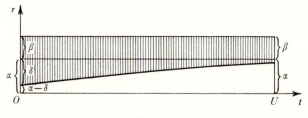

Fig. 26

increase in employment will now fall from $\delta + \beta$ at the beginning of the period to β at its end. (See Fig. 26.)

The role of the labour reserve here is to make possible a compensation for the fall in the rate of increase in productivity (which amounts to $\alpha - \delta$ at the beginning of the period OU) by a correspondingly higher rate of increase in employment. The gain derived here from drawing upon the labour reserve is the higher relative share of consumption in the national income, which raises the *level* of consumption throughout the period considered while its rate of growth, as well as that of the national income, is unchanged at the level $\alpha + \beta$.

At the end of the period OU drawing on the labour reserve will cease because the rate of increase in productivity will have returned to the level α. If by that time the labour reserve has been exhausted then, in contrast to the case previously considered, this will not affect the rate of growth at all since this is based solely on the increase in productivity resulting from technical progress (at a rate α) and on the natural increase in the labour force (at a rate β).

As may be seen, in the case presently considered the labour reserve permits a once-for-all increase in the standard of living rather than a higher rate of growth of consumption (*pari passu* with national income) over the period OU.

It is, of course, possible that the government will choose a variant which is intermediate between the two variants considered above, represented by point T on the curve GH lying between G and H (see Fig. 25). In such a case there will be an increase in both the rate of growth and the relative share of consumption in the national income over the period OU, for the ordinate of T is higher than $\alpha + \beta$ and its abscissa is lower than $i_0 = OA$ (this means that the relative share of productive accumulation in the national income will be lower, and that of consumption higher, than in the basic position represented by point B). It is clear, however, that the increase in the rate of growth will be smaller than in the first variant and the rise in the relative share of consumption in the national income will be less pronounced than in the second.

11. THE STRUCTURE OF INVESTMENT

1. So far we have laid the main stress in our discussion on changes in the relative share of productive accumulation (and in particular of productive investment) in the national income. In the case of uniform growth this share remains constant. It rises in the case of accelerated growth of national income, e.g. in the 'transition period' where the rate of growth is increased gradually with real wages remaining constant. Finally, when the rate of growth decreases – as in the period of 'recasting' aimed at overcoming a labour shortage – the relative shares of productive accumulation and of productive investment in the national income decline. We shall now deal with the problem of changes in the structure of investment which result from such redistributions of the national income. More specifically, there arises the question, what part of total productive investment, I, is allocated in different cases to the investment sector itself – i.e. to the sector which produces productive equipment? We shall denote this part by I_i. To begin with, it is clear that with uniform growth the relative share of total investment devoted to the investment sector, i.e. I_i/I, remains constant. In such a case both total investment and national income increase at the same constant rate; stocks of capital equipment in the investment and non-investment† sectors bear a constant relation to each other and, as they grow at the same rate, the ratio between investment outlays in each of them must also remain constant.

Furthermore, the higher the rate of growth and thus – given the constancy of the parameters m, a and u – the higher the relative share of investment in national income I/Y, the higher must also be the relative share of the investment sector in total

---

† This sector covers consumption in the broad sense and the increase in inventories.

investment I_i/I. For if both the investment and non-investment sectors are to expand at a constant rate, to a higher I/Y there must also correspond a higher proportion of total investment in the investment sector.

When I/Y is increased to a higher level – as happens in the 'transition period' – I_i/I must rise correspondingly. But *in the course* of such a process the proportion I_i/I must rise still more, since in this period the rate of growth of investment is higher than that of national income (the relative share of investment in the national income I/Y being raised) which means a more rapid expansion of the investment sector than of other sectors of production.

It should be noted that the above argument rests upon the assumption that equipment used for producing investment goods is qualitatively different from that used for producing other goods, and thus any increase in investment necessarily involves an expansion of the investment sector. This assumption is obviously not entirely realistic, as in many cases the same equipment can be used to produce goods for various end uses and, in particular, changes in the relative share of investment in the national income can be effected to some extent through foreign trade. We shall return to this subject towards the end of the present chapter, but in the meantime we shall assume in our argument that no increase in investment is possible without an expansion of the productive capacity of the investment sector. In particular, we shall disregard foreign trade.

2. Before we enter into a more detailed discussion on the subject of the relative share of I_i in total investment I, we still have to say a few words about the capital–output ratio in the investment sector as compared with the corresponding ratio for the economy as a whole.

At the start of this book we made the assumption that the capital–output ratio for total investment m did not depend upon the structure of investment. Strictly speaking this assumption can be satisfied only if the capital–output ratio in the investment sector is equal to the ratio in the non-investment sector. It will, however, also be approximately satisfied when the difference between the ratios for both sectors (including production of the respective raw materials) is not very large, and such is in fact the case.† As will be seen below, under such conditions even rather sizeable changes in the structure of investment affect m only slightly.

The relationship between m for the economy as a whole, m_i for the investment sector, and m_c for the remainder of the economy is as follows:

$$\frac{1}{m}I = \frac{1}{m_i}I_i + \frac{1}{m_c}(I - I_i)$$

where I_i denotes, as above, investment in the investment sector. Dividing both sides of the equation by total investment I we obtain

$$\frac{1}{m} = \frac{1}{m_i}\frac{I_i}{I} + \frac{1}{m_c}\frac{I - I_i}{I}$$

Let us assume $m_i = 3$ and $m_c = 2$; then, for $I_i/I = 0.1$ we obtain $m = 2.1$ and for $I_i/I = 0.5$ we obtain $m = 2.4$. The results of our subsequent argument will not be significantly affected if we assume that m remains constant at the level of 2.25.

We shall thus assume below that m is sufficiently stable to permit us to disregard changes resulting from shifts in the structure of investment.‡ At the same time, however, we shall take into account the difference between the capital–output ratio in the investment sector m_i and the overall ratio m, this difference being a significant factor in the distribution of investment between the investment and non-investment sector.

3. We shall now examine in detail the changes in I_i/I which result from changes in the level of I/Y. Let us begin by recalling equation (3) which shows the relationship between the rate of growth of national income and the relative share of productive investment in the national income:

$$r = \frac{1}{m}\frac{I}{Y} - (a - u)$$

† In contrast, primary production is generally characterized by a much higher capital–output ratio than manufacturing.
‡ With the exception of one extreme case which is considered towards the end of the present chapter.

Structure of investment

Let us now denote by r_i the rate of growth of productive investment. We may write an equation similar to (3) for the investment sector alone. If we include in this sector the output of all raw materials which are used in the production of investment goods the income produced in this sector is equal to I.† Productive investment in this sector was denoted above by I_i; assuming for the sake of simplicity that a and u for this sector are the same as for the economy as a whole, may may write

$$r_i = \frac{1}{m_i} \frac{I_i}{I} - (a - u) \qquad (33)$$

We now subtract equation (3) from equation (33):

$$r_i - r = \frac{1}{m_i} \frac{I_i}{I} - \frac{1}{m} \frac{I}{Y}$$

Hence we obtain the formula

$$\frac{I_i}{I} = \frac{m_i}{m} \frac{I}{Y} + m_i(r_i - r) \qquad (34)$$

which we shall apply to the examination of changes in I_i/I under different circumstances.

In the case of uniform growth both r and I/Y are constant. Since the latter is constant, I grows at the same rate as Y (i.e. at the rate r) which means that $r_i = r$. Therefore, according to equation (34), in this case we have

$$\frac{I_i}{I} = \frac{m_i}{m} \frac{I}{Y} \qquad (35)$$

It follows that I_i/I is constant, as is I/Y. Moreover, to a greater relative share of investment in the national income there corresponds a proportionately higher relative share of the investment sector in total investment I_i/I. If the capital–output ratio in the investment sector m_i is equal to the overall capital–output ratio m, we have

$$\frac{I_i}{I} = \frac{I}{Y}$$

Let us now consider the case of accelerating growth where both r and I/Y are increasing. The increase in the latter means that

† As noted above we disregard foreign trade for the time being.

A socialist economy

investment grows more rapidly than national income – i.e. $r_i > r$. From this and from equation (34) it follows that

$$\frac{I_i}{I} > \frac{m_i}{m}\frac{I}{Y} \tag{36}$$

Thus the relative share of the investment sector in total investment corresponding to a given level of I/Y is greater here than it would be in the case of uniform growth (this will be seen by comparing formulae (35) and (36). For the special case when $m_i = m$ we have the inequality

$$\frac{I_i}{I} > \frac{I}{Y}$$

Let us suppose that in the initial position the economy is subject to uniform growth. We have, then, the relationship

$$\frac{I_{i,0}}{I_0} = \frac{m_i}{m}\frac{I_0}{Y_0} \tag{37}$$

where Y_0, I_0 and $I_{i,0}$ are, respectively, the national income, productive investment and investment in the investment sector, at the point of departure of the accelerated growth. After a period of τ years of such growth we enter a new period of uniform growth, but with a higher rate of growth of national income (cf. Chapter 4, section 5). Let us write Y_τ, I_τ, $I_{i,\tau}$ for national income, productive investment and investment in the investment sector, at the beginning of the new period of uniform growth. Again we have the relationship

$$\frac{I_{i,\tau}}{I_\tau} = \frac{m_i}{m}\frac{I_\tau}{Y_\tau} \tag{38}$$

Evidently, I_τ/Y_τ is higher than the corresponding ratio in the initial position corresponding to the higher r. As will be seen from formula (38), the ratio $I_{i,\tau}/I_\tau$ is proportionately higher as well. But *during* the period of acceleration the relationship between I_i/I and I/Y will be different, for at time t it follows from formula (34) that

$$\frac{I_{i,t}}{I_t} = \frac{m_i}{m}\frac{I_t}{Y_t} + m_i(r_{i,t} - r_t)$$

106

where $I_{i,t}$, I_t, Y_t, $r_{i,t}$ and r_t are respectively investment in the investment sector, total investment, national income, and the rates of growth of investment and of national income – all at time t within the transition period ($0 < t < \tau$).

From the above equation we subtract equation (37) and thus obtain

$$\frac{I_{i,t}}{I_t} - \frac{I_{i,0}}{I_0} = \frac{m_i}{m}\left(\frac{I_t}{Y_t} - \frac{I_0}{Y_0}\right) + m_i(r_{i,t} - r_t)$$

Consequently the increase in I_i/I from the beginning of the transition period to time t depends not only on a corresponding increase in I/Y but also on the difference between the rates of growth of investment and national income. This growth of I_i/I reflects the fact that the fixed capital in the investment sector is expanded more rapidly than that in the remainder of the economy.

When the transition period is over and a new period of uniform growth begins, the term $m_i(r_{i,t} - r_t)$ obviously disappears so that at time τ we have

$$\frac{I_{i,\tau}}{I_\tau} - \frac{I_{i,0}}{I_0} = \frac{m_i}{m}\left(\frac{I_\tau}{Y_\tau} - \frac{I_0}{Y_0}\right)$$

which also follows directly from formulae (37) and (38).

When growth is slowed down – as, for example, in a period of 'recasting' aimed at overcoming the shortage of labour – the situation is reversed: I_i/I is smaller than $(m_i/m)(I/Y)$ in the period of slowing down of growth.

4. It may be shown on the basis of formula (34) that there exists a ceiling to the deviation of the rate of growth of investment from that of national income which is determined by the productive capacity of the investment sector. The greater this deviation, the greater must be the relative share of the investment sector in total investment, i.e. I_i/I. This share, however, cannot exceed unity since *gross* investment in the non-investment sector cannot become negative. Assuming $I_i/I = 1$ we obtain from

formula (34) the following expression for the case where $r_i - r$ reaches a maximum:

$$1 = \frac{m_i}{m}\frac{I}{Y} + m_i(r_i - r)$$

This formula, however, is not quite correct. As a first approximation we based our argument in this chapter on a constant m which, however, differed from m_i. But in the extreme case presently considered m becomes equal to m_i since total investment is concentrated in the investment sector. Accordingly, we can make our formula more precise by substituting m_i for m; we thus obtain

$$1 = \frac{Y}{I} + m_i(r_i - r)$$

or

$$r_i - r = \frac{1}{m_i}\left(1 - \frac{I}{Y}\right) \tag{39}$$

If we assume $m_i = 3$ and $I/Y \geqslant 0.2$, the maximum possible value of $r_i - r$ will be less than $(1 - 0.2)/3$, or less than 26.5 per cent.†

It follows that when a decision is being taken on the acceleration of the growth of national income, it must be ascertained that the ceiling to the difference between the rate of growth of investment and that of national income is not exceeded in the course of this acceleration – i.e. in the 'transition period'. In fact this is rather unlikely to be the case under our assumption of constancy of real wages which is tantamount to consumption rising *pari passu* with employment in the 'transition period'. When the ceiling of $r_i - r$ is reached all investment will be concentrated in the investment sector and the production of the non-investment sector will change at a rate $u - a$. Thus in order to maintain real wages u would have to be rather high. If, however, such a situation does arise, $r_i - r$ must be reduced by slowing down the acceleration of growth and thus lengthening the 'transition period'. This could be accomplished by permitting real wages to increase somewhat, instead of keeping them

---

† If we use formula (34) without modification and assume $m = 2.25$ we obtain 24.5 per cent for the maximum of $r_i - r$.

stable (of course, their growth would have to be less rapid than that of labour productivity resulting from technical progress).

5. So far we have ignored the possibility of increasing investment either by changing the way in which some equipment is used, or through foreign trade (e.g. the possibility of turning plant used in the manufacture of consumer durables to production of machinery, or increasing imports of machinery at the expense of either cutting down imports of consumer goods or increasing exports of these goods). Hence the only way of increasing the relative share of investment in the national income was to make the investment sector expand more rapidly than total productive capacity. Now we shall also take into account the possibility of changes in the use made of this capacity, and in the structure of foreign trade.

So far the rate of growth of investment has been determined by the formula

$$r_i = \frac{1}{m_i} \frac{I_i}{I} - (a - u) \tag{33}$$

which is equivalent to

$$\Delta I = \frac{1}{m_i} I_i - aI + uI \tag{39'}$$

The increment of investment ΔI thus depends on: the productive effect of investment I_i in the investment sector; the contraction of income aI produced in this sector as a result of obsolescence and wear and tear of equipment; and the increase in income uI resulting from improvements in the utilization of equipment.[†]

This formula is no longer adequate for the problem. Suppose investment is to grow more rapidly than national income – i.e. that $r_i I > rI$. The expression $r_i I - rI$ represents the part of the increment in investment which is responsible for the increase in the relative share of investment in the national income. It must now be taken into account that part of $r_i I - rI$ results from the

---

† As we are no longer ignoring foreign trade, it follows that, to make the part of national income produced in the investment sector equal to the value of investment *I*, we must include in this sector that part of total production for export which covers payment for imports both of raw materials for the investment sector and of finished investment goods (machinery, etc.).

change in the use made of capital equipment, or in the structure of foreign trade. Let us suppose that this change is $d(r_i - r)I$, where d is a coefficient $\leqslant 1$. Instead of formula (33) we may now write

$$\Delta I = \frac{1}{m_i} I_i - (a-u)I + d(r_i - r)I$$

or, dividing both sides by I,

$$\frac{\Delta I}{I} = r_i = \frac{1}{m_i}\frac{I_i}{I} - (a-u) + d(r_i - r) \tag{40}$$

When $r_i = r$ the additional term on the right-hand side of the equation disappears; this is as it should be since $r_i = r$ means that the economy is expanding at a constant rate r and no change in the rate of investment is needed on account of changes in the use made of capital equipment or in the structure of foreign trade.

If the equation

$$r = \frac{1}{m}\frac{I}{Y} - (a-u) \tag{3}$$

is deducted from equation (40) we obtain

$$r_i - r = \frac{1}{m_i}\cdot\frac{I_i}{I} - \frac{1}{m}\frac{I}{Y} + d(r_i - r)$$

or

$$\frac{I_i}{I} = \frac{m_i}{m}\cdot\frac{I}{Y} + m_i(1-d)(r_i - r) \tag{41}$$

This equation corresponds to equation (34) while differing from it in that the coefficient of $r_i - r$ has now been reduced from m_i to $m_i(1-d)$. This means that the relative share of investment in the investment sector in total investment I corresponding to a given difference $r_i - r$ is now smaller, because a faster expansion of the investment sector is no longer the only method used to increase the relative share of investment in the national income when the growth of the latter is to be accelerated.

However, in the case of uniform growth, when $r_i = r$, we have the old formula (35)

$$\frac{I_i}{I} = \frac{m_i}{m}\frac{I}{Y}$$

because in this case there is no question of increasing the share of investment in the national income.

Finally, for the ceiling value of $r_i - r$ which is reached in the situation when $I_i = I$ and $m = m_i$, we obtain from formula (41) the equation

$$r_i - r = \frac{1}{m_i(1 - d)}\left(1 - \frac{I}{Y}\right) \tag{42}$$

which, again, differs from formula (39) in that the term $m_i(1 - d)$ replaces m_i in the denominator of the right-hand side of the equation. As a result, the ceiling for $r_i - r$ now becomes higher than it was in the former case. This results from the fact that the limiting influence of the productive capacity of the investment sector on the difference between r_i and r is now relaxed; the more rapid increase in investment than that in the national income is partly achieved by changes in favour of investment in the use of equipment and in the structure of foreign trade.

APPENDIX

THE PRODUCTION CURVE AND THE EVALUATION OF THE EFFICIENCY OF INVESTMENT IN A SOCIALIST ECONOMY

[1967]

1. The concept of the production curve is based on the assumption of an equal life-span for all types of equipment, since only in such a case can a variant for producing a given increment of national income be fully characterized by the investment outlay and the labour force associated with it (the third characteristic being the life-span of equipment). But even taking this assumption for granted the approach to the production curve developed in Chapter 7, section 2 may be questioned (cf. note †, p. 53). For the central planning authorities are obviously unable to consider the enormous number of possible variants capable of producing an increment in the national income in order to eliminate those which are absolutely inferior (i.e. for which the investment outlays are greater and the labour force not less than in some other variant or vice versa). Thus the production curve appears to be purely theoretical in character since its points are not necessarily realized in practice (i.e. one cannot exclude the possibility that a definitely inefficient variant may be selected). We shall, however, show that this problem does not arise if the evaluation of the efficiency of investment for any type of commodity is based on the criterion

$$\frac{j}{T} + w = \text{minimum}$$

Appendix

where j is total investment outlay taken over all stages of production, w total current costs (exclusive of depreciation), and T the so-called recoupment period.† Indeed, we shall prove that to a given T there corresponds a point on the production curve. It should be pointed out that on the assumption of an equal life-span for all types of equipment the simple condition

$$\frac{j}{T} + w = \text{minimum}$$

is an appropriate criterion for the choice of variants.

We shall assume that in the case where the 'joint investment and labour outlay' $j/T + w$ is equal for two variants the less capital intensive one is chosen – i.e. that with a smaller j.

We denote by j_c and w_c the investment outlay and costs of the variant of production chosen for a given type of commodity and by j and w these parameters for any variant for this type of commodity. We then have

$$\frac{j_c}{T} + w_c \leqslant \frac{j}{T} + w$$

By adding these inequalities for the economy as a whole we obtain

$$\Sigma \left(\frac{j_c}{T} + w_c \right) \leqslant \Sigma \left(\frac{j}{T} + w \right)$$

or
$$\frac{1}{T}\Sigma j_c + \Sigma w_c \leqslant \frac{1}{T}\Sigma j + \Sigma w \qquad (43)$$

Σj_c and Σw_c, however, are the aggregate investment outlay J_c, and aggregate costs W_c required for a given increase in national

† [In the planning practice of East-European countries, the 'recoupment period' is a parameter fixed by the Planning Commission in instructions issued to enterprises and project-making organizations. It is defined as the number of years over which the *additional* investment expenditure associated with the project selected – in comparison with the immediately less investment-intensive project available to reach the same planned target – *must* be 'recouped' by means of lower yearly operating costs. The observance of this rule is tantamount to the use of a shadow capital charge. In the economic reforms that have been taking place in Eastern Europe this rule is being gradually replaced by the introduction of actual payments of interest and capital charges by firms, and straightforward discounting methods. *D.M.N.*]

income using the methods actually adopted, while Σj and Σw are the aggregate values J and W for any other variant. We thus have

$$\frac{J_c}{T} + W_c \leqslant \frac{J}{T} + W \qquad (43')$$

It follows directly that the point J_c, W_c cannot correspond to an absolutely inferior variant. Indeed, if J_c were, for instance, greater than J' for some other variant, and W_c were no less than W', we could write

$$\frac{J'}{T} + W' < \frac{J_c}{T} + W_c$$

which would contradict inequality $(43')$.

Let us now denote the hourly wage for unskilled labour by h. To aggregate costs W_c there corresponds a labour force expressed in terms of unskilled labour $L_c = W_c/h$. It follows from the above that the point J_c, L_c is situated on the production curve because the latter represents all the 'efficient' variants for producing a given increase in national income (i.e. the variants which are not absolutely inferior).

J_c, L_c is a point on the production curve corresponding to a given period of recoupment T; it will be noticed that the greater is T, the further to the right on the production curve is the corresponding point J_c, L_c–because a higher recoupment period 'lets in' more capital-intensive and less labour-intensive variants for particular types of commodity. However, we shall not be satisfied with this rather intuitive argument, but shall prove the theorem rigorously and at the same time demonstrate that the production curve is concave.

2. Let us start with a diagrammatic representation of the variants of production for a given type of commodity, plotting investment outlays j as the abscissa, and the current costs w as the ordinate (Fig. 27).

If the recoupment period is T, it can be shown that the best variant will be on the lowest possible straight line of slope $-1/T$.

The equation for the straight line with such a slope is

$$w = -\frac{j}{T} + b$$

where b is the distance from the origin of the point of intersection of this straight line with the j-axis. Thus

$$\frac{j}{T} + w = b$$

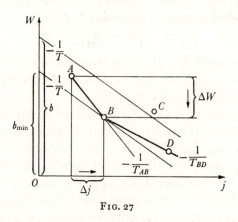

FIG. 27

and the condition for the best variant is

$$\frac{j}{T} + w = b_{\text{minimum}}$$

It follows directly that a point j, w must be chosen through which there passes the straight line with the lowest b. It also follows that at no T is point C considered, and there remain only A, B, D on the lower concave boundary from which to choose. Let us now denote the recoupment periods corresponding to the slopes AB and BD by T_{AB} and T_{BD}. If $T = T_{AB}$ we shall choose variant A; indeed for variants A and B the value of the expression $j/T + w$ is the same and according to our rule we then choose the less capital-intensive variant. If $T_{AB} < T \leqslant T_{BD}$ we choose variant B (the case represented in Fig. 27). Finally, when $T > T_{BD}$, variant D will prove the best. In other words if when increasing the recoupment period T we exceed the level T_{AB}, we shift from

8-2

the variant A to a more capital-intensive and less labour-intensive variant B. (If we exceed T_{BD} we shift correspondingly from variant B to variant D.)

3. Let us now consider all the types of commodity for which we may draw diagrams similar to Fig. 27. Let us derive from each diagram the recoupment periods T corresponding to the segments of the lower concave boundary such as T_{AB} and T_{BD}. Let us range all these recoupment periods according to their length; we shall obtain an increasing sequence

$$T_1, T_2, ..., T_s, \quad T_{s+1}, ..., T_m.$$

It should be noted that T_s may correspond to a number of types of commodity and that T_{s+1} may obviously correspond to different types of commodity from T_s.

Let us imagine that a recoupment period T_s has been adopted corresponding to the point J_s, L_s on the production curve and that we next pass from T_s to T_{s+1}. Then for types of commodity to which T_s corresponds, this level of the recoupment period will be exceeded (for instance T_{AB} on Fig. 27) and, according to the above, a shift will occur for these commodities to more capital- and less labour-intensive variants (for instance from variant A to variant B). As a result the value of the investment outlay in the economy as a whole will also increase from J_s to the higher level J_{s+1}, and the labour force required will fall from L_s to L_{s+1}. The point J_{s+1}, L_{s+1} on the curve of production corresponding to T_{s+1}, will therefore be situated to the right of and below the point J_s, L_s which corresponds to T_s (see Fig. 28).

Nor is this all, for T_s corresponds to a segment of the lower boundary of the set of points representing the variants on one or more diagrams relating to particular types of commodity (for instance AB in Fig. 27). When T_s is exceeded a shift occurs from the left-hand end of this segment to the right-hand end (e.g. from A to B). Thus the respective increases in current costs Δw and investment Δj are in the ratio $-1/T_s$ (e.g. $-1/T_{AB}$), i.e.

$$\Delta w = -\frac{1}{T_s} \Delta j$$

Since the sum of these increases constitutes the increment in aggregate investment outlay and aggregate costs, we obtain

$$W_{s+1} - W_s = -\frac{1}{T_s}(J_{s+1} - J_s)$$

and thus $$L_{s+1} - L_s = -\frac{1}{hT_s}(J_{s+1} - J_s) \qquad (44)$$

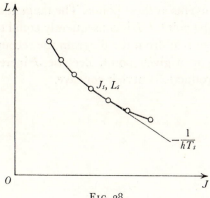

Fig. 28

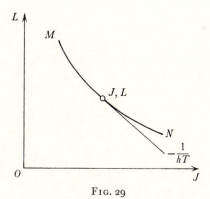

Fig. 29

It follows directly that the straight line connecting the subsequent points J_s, L_s and J_{s+1}, L_{s+1} situated on the curve of production has a slope $-1/hT_s$. In other words the segment starting from the point J_s, L_s has the slope $-1/hT_s$ (Fig. 28). Consequently, the greater the recoupment period T_s, the further to the right is situated the corresponding point J_s, L_s (which has already been proved above) and the smaller the slope of the segment starting from this point. This means, however, that the line represented on Fig. 28 is concave.

If the points J_s, L_s are sufficiently close to each other this line approaches the production curve and the slopes of its segments – those of the tangents at these points. The tangent of the production curve at the point J, L is consequently equal to $-1/hT$ and thus it is easy to read from the diagram the recoupment period corresponding to a given point. Because J increases together with T, the production curve is concave.

PART II

INVESTMENT PLANNING AND
PROJECT SELECTION

12. THE SCOPE OF THE EVALUATION OF THE EFFICIENCY OF INVESTMENT IN A SOCIALIST ECONOMY
[1970]

1. The efficiency of investment is evaluated in principle in the socialist centrally planned economies for two purposes: (*a*) the comparison of different technological variants for the achievement of the same productive target; (*b*) the comparison of different possibilities of obtaining the amounts of foreign currencies necessary to cover import requirements, either by means of exports or by means of national production aimed at import substitution.

It is often said, not only in the West but also in the socialist countries, that such application of the calculus of effectiveness has too limited a character, because it leaves, it seems, the general directions of development of the economy to the arbitrary decisions of the planning authorities. We shall try to show here that such contentions are based on a misunderstanding. (It is true that the evaluation of investment efficiency could still be enlarged to include the determination of the consumption structure, but this is a problem much more complex than the two mentioned above, since it requires the definition of equivalence of two consumption aggregates of different structure; see section 3 below.)

2. Let us begin by considering a fictional, but nonetheless

instructive situation. Let us imagine, namely, a closed economy in which there are no technological alternatives, i.e. each productive target can be achieved in one way only. Let us assume further that in the perspective plan the planning authorities have determined the growth path of national income through time (measured at constant prices) and also the structure of consumption and unproductive investment, as well as the relation among these magnitudes in each year of the plan.

It can be seen easily that in such conditions there exists only one balanced-plan variant. The volume and structure of investment are determined by the planned growth of national income, and so are the structure of consumption and unproductive investment, and the relation between these two magnitudes. Suppose for instance that consumption is at a level higher than in the plan so constructed. Then, since the relation between consumption and unproductive investment is given, the structure and volume of investment also have to be adjusted, and for a given national income less is left for productive accumulation and the increase in circulating capital. The lower level of these magnitudes, in turn, without the possibility of technical choice and the operation of international trade, and also for a determined structure of consumption and unproductive investment, cannot in any way be sufficient to achieve the increase of national income assumed in the plan.

Not only cannot the volume of investment undergo change with respect to the plan constructed, but neither can its structure, because again the assumptions made would not allow the achievement of the assumed structure of consumption and unproductive investment. This means that in a situation where there is no problem of choice of production techniques nor of foreign-trade variants, once the planning authorities have determined the time path of national income, the structure of consumption and unproductive investment, the problem of evaluation of investment efficiency does not arise.

Together with the possibility of choice of techniques and of various patterns of foreign trade, two degrees of freedom arise, and indeed it is within the framework of these degrees that the evaluation of investment efficiency can operate – given the assumptions made by the planning authorities about the growth rate of national income, the structure of consumption and unproductive investment.

3. In practice we are faced exactly with such a situation. The plan should really be constructed for several hypothetical paths of national income growth, and the planning authorities should choose among them; and given the conflict between consumption in the short and the long run that usually arises, this choice contains elements of political character. By constructing each of the plans corresponding to hypothesis in the field of growth paths, a given structure of consumption and unproductive investment is assumed more or less in a discretionary way: either the consumption at the end of the plan is patterned on the more developed countries and interpolations are made for the intermediate years; or the income elasticities of demand for different commodities, taken from family budgets, are used as guidelines; or, finally, both methods are used at the same time in order to formulate a view about this problem, and then take the final decision about it.

As we have already said (in section 1 above) the calculus of investment effectiveness could be extended to include the problem of choice of the 'cheapest' consumption structure. Then we must introduce the criterion of equivalence of two different consumption aggregates. A first step in this direction is contained in my paper 'On optimum consumption structure',† where I have also outlined a method for the choice of consumption structure in the perspective plan. My preliminary ideas, however, have not yet reached either a general solution, or a practical application. Therefore we still take the decision about the structure of consumption (and unproductive investment) as given in the plan variants corresponding to different growth rates.

4. In such conditions, the field in which we assess the efficiency

† *Gospodarka Planowa*, 1963.

of investment is, as we have said above, the choice of techniques for the achievement of given productive targets and the pattern of exports and imports. The task of the evaluation of efficiency understood in this way is the achievement of the minimum investment consistent with the maintenance of equilibrium in the balance of the labour force and the balance of payments. In other words, for a given value of exports that covers (together with possible foreign loans) the value of imports, investment should be fixed at the lowest level at which the full employment of the labour force is obtained. A lower level of investment would mean that the plan is unrealistic, given the unemployment of labour. A higher level of investment would in turn imply a waste of resources that would negatively affect consumption.

From this argument, on the other hand, one should not draw the conclusion that the investment calculus can by itself determine completely the pattern of foreign trade or even the productive techniques. An obstacle to obtaining the most effective export pattern can appear due, from the supply side, to technical-organisational factors limiting the growth rate of particular branches, and from the side of demand, to the insufficient absorption capacity of foreign markets. The export pattern is most effective when the rate of its expansion is low. Also, even the application of some effective technology can meet long-term bottlenecks. For instance, the burning of oil is more effective than the burning of coal, but in Poland that depends on the import of crude oil, and therefore it raises the foreign trade difficulties mentioned above.

If we take into account this set of problems, then it appears that the necessary investment is in principle higher than the level which we would obtain by applying the 'pure' evaluation of investment efficiency.

5. It is also worth further illustrating the arguments above, by using them to answer the frequent question whether manufacturing industries should not be developed, because of their lower capital intensity, rather than primary industries producing

raw materials. If we treat the question independently of foreign trade considerations, it really makes no sense at all. We cannot produce machines rather than copper, since that leads to a surplus of machines and a deficit of copper.

Only if this problem is considered within the context of foreign trade can an answer to it be found in the calculus of investment efficiency. This calculus can in fact show that it is more advantageous to produce machines for export and to import copper in exchange, rather than produce copper at home. But even this, in the light of the considerations of section 4 above, still does not prejudge the issue. The point is that it is not necessarily feasible for the export of machines to be expanded in order to import copper, and we might have to sell the machines so cheaply that this becomes ineffective. Therefore the construction of a copper mine, regardless of its capital intensity, can turn out to be, in the end, an appropriate way of implementing the development plan of the economy.

Generally speaking, the so-called problem of the 'directions of development' makes sense only when it is treated as the choice of the pattern of foreign trade (as well as the production technology), because only then does it not lead to plan imbalance. Once the problem is formulated in this way, it *can* be solved by means of the calculus of investment efficiency, provided allowance is made for the absorption capacity of foreign markets for different export goods, and for the technical-organizational barriers to the development of the production of particular branches.

13. BASIC PROBLEMS IN THE THEORY OF THE EFFICIENCY OF INVESTMENT

[1970]

PART I. A SIMPLIFIED MODEL

1. Let there be a given closed national economy consisting of branches representing different stages in the production of an end product. For each of these branches there is an established plan of development for a long period o, T at constant rates of growth r (T is the same for all the branches). The growth rates r are, as a rule, different for the different branches. In addition, the plan provides for a constant coefficient of scrapping a for each branch: in the interval t, $t + dt$ the volume of production P_t is reduced as a result of the scrapping of old equipment characterized by the highest expenditure of live labour† by $a P_t dt$, where P_t is the production of the given branch at the moment t. No changes occur in the existing productive apparatus before modernization other than those due to the scrapping of old equipment. Consequently, the growth of production by $r P_t dt$ is a result of the new production $(r + a) P_t dt$ arising from investment and the scrapping of old equipment, which reduced productive capacity by $a P_t dt$.

The total volume of production at the new capacity $(r + a) P_t$ may be realized by different investment variants representing different techniques, i.e. by different combinations of investment outlays (expressed in constant prices) and expenditure on live labour (expressed in constant wages). The variants to choose from are, of course, subject to changes as a result of technical progress:

---

† ['live' labour = labour directly used in current production, as opposed to labour 'crystallized' or 'stored up' in capital goods. *D.M.N.*]

new variants displace old ones, which become absolutely ineffective, i.e. variants in which capital investment is higher and labour costs are no lower than in the other variants or vice versa.

Technical progress in the use of materials is left out of consideration. It is assumed that the variants compared over a given period do not differ with regard to expenditure on materials. This corresponds to the premise that there is a fixed programme for the development of all branches, some of which produce materials for the others. (It will be assumed that the plan is balanced from the point of view of the consumption of materials.)†

The amount of capital investment arising from the choice of variant will, as a rule, differ from the production of investment goods adopted in the initial plan. We shall however assume that the necessary changes of proportion between investment and consumption may be made without serious disturbance to the development plans of the individual branches by making full use of the growth of the labour force.

2. Let us denote by i_t the investment intensity of the production $(r+a)P_t dt$, and the labour intensity by c_t. At the time t the separate variants may be represented by different combinations of i_t and c_t. Let us denote the highest labour intensity of the output produced with the existing equipment by x_t, and the growth in labour costs in the entire branch by $\rho_t P_t dt$. We then have

$$(r+a)P_t dt . c_t - aP_t dt . x_t = \rho_t P_t dt \qquad (1)$$

or $$P_t c_t dt - aPt_t(x_t - c_t)dt = \rho P_t dt \qquad (1')$$

The first term in the left side of equation $(1')$ represents the expenditure on live labour which when taken in conjunction with the corresponding investment will make it possible to increase the production of the branch P_t by $rP_t dt$; the second

† This is completely incompatible with the assumption made above that there is uniform growth of the individual branches at rates which are, as a rule, different. The present assumption is made as a first approximation to a materially balanced plan.

term represents the saving in expenditure on live labour achieved as a result of the capital investment $a P_t i_t dt$ which replaces the scrapped productive capacity.

The investment per unit of increment of production is

$$i_t(r+a)/r,$$

and the labour costs in the entire branch per unit of this increment are, in accordance with formula (1),

$$\frac{\rho_t}{r} = c_t \frac{r+a}{r} - x_t \frac{a}{r} \tag{1''}$$

It should be noted that as long as scrapping affects only items existing at time o, the quantity x_t is determined for a given initial state of the branch by the growth rate of production r and by the scrapping coefficient a. Conversely, i_t and c_t are to be selected from the variants existing at time t. However, when equipment installed in the period o, ..., T begins to be scrapped, the quantity x_t will not be *fully* determined by r and a, since it is also dependent on the choice of production technique already made in the period o, T.

Let us denote the sum $\Sigma(r+a) P_t i_t dt$ for all branches by $I_t dt$. I_t is therefore the aggregate productive investment of the entire system in the interval t, $t+dt$ in unit time. The sum $\Sigma \rho_t P_t dt$ is the additional demand for labour of all branches, which equals the growth in the aggregate expenditure on live labour (expressed in constant wages) in the interval t, $t+dt$. We denote this quantity in unit time by W_t.

3. Let us now consider the problem of the minimization of aggregate investment I_t for a given increase in the labour force at a moment t of the period o, T. It is assumed in the first stage of the analysis that the quantity x_t is known. In the next stage it is proved that this condition is not essential, given certain further simplifications. It is demonstrated that the volume of investment determined by the method proposed by us will evidently be approximately equal to the minimum at all times t in the period o, T with the coefficients r and a assigned for all branches and

with the given dynamics of the aggregate increment of the labour force.

We start by assuming that the index of the efficiency of investment is a linear function of investment and expenditure on live labour per unit of the increment of production $r P_t dt$

$$E_t = \epsilon . i_t \frac{r+a}{r} + \left(c_t \frac{r+a}{r} - x_t \frac{a}{r} \right) \qquad (2)$$

where ϵ is a positive parameter which is the same for all branches. We proceed by choosing for a given ϵ a variant of i_t, c_t on the basis of the criterion

$$E_t = \min \qquad (3)$$

and should E_t be the same for two variants we select the one for which i_t is lower. When x_t, a and r are given, this criterion is equivalent to

$$\epsilon i_t + c_t = \min \qquad (4)$$

Let us denote the optimal variant by i'_t, c'_t and the corresponding index of efficiency by E_t. We then have

$$E'_t \leqslant E'_t \qquad (5)$$

Taking the sum over the branches we have

$$\Sigma E'_t r P_t dt \leqslant \Sigma E_t r P_t dt$$

and it follows, in accordance with (1″) and (2), that

$$\epsilon \Sigma (r+a) P_t i'_t + E \rho'_t P_t \leqslant \epsilon \Sigma (r+a) P_t i_t + \Sigma \rho_t P_t$$

or

$$\epsilon I'_t + W'_t \leqslant \epsilon I_t + W_t \qquad (6)$$

where I'_t and W'_t correspond to the variants which are optimal for each branch on the basis of the criterion (3) or (4).

4. A change in the parameter ϵ affects the choice of investment variant. If in some branch there is an E'_t corresponding to ϵ which is equal to the E_t for another, more investment-intensive variant, an arbitrarily small reduction of ϵ will lead to the choice of this latter variant. In fact, the indices of the efficiency of investment will then be $E'_t - \Delta \epsilon i'_t$ and $E_t - \Delta \epsilon i_t$. The second of these indices is less than the first because

$$E'_t = E_t \quad \text{and} \quad i'_t < i_t.$$

Investment planning

Thus at certain values of ϵ_k arranged in increasing order, I'_t and W'_t will alter when there is the slightest reduction of ϵ: whereas $I'_{t,k}$ and $W'_{t,k}$ correspond to ϵ_k, what corresponds to $E_k - \Delta\epsilon$ is already $I'_{t,k-1} > I'_{t,k}$ and $W_{t,k-1} < W'_{t,k}$. It follows that $I_{t,k}$ is a decreasing sequence and $W_{t,k}$ an increasing one.

It follows from (6) that

$$(\epsilon_k - \Delta\epsilon) I'_{t,k-1} + W'_{t,k-1} \leqslant (\epsilon_k - \Delta\epsilon) I'_{t,k} + W'_{t,k}$$

and
$$\epsilon_k I'_{t,k} + W'_{t,k} \leqslant \epsilon_k I'_{t,k-1} + W'_{t,k-1}$$

Taking into consideration $I'_{t,k-1} > I'_{t,k}$, we obtain

$$\epsilon_k - \Delta\epsilon \leqslant \frac{W'_{t,k} - W'_{t,k-1}}{I'_{t,k-1} - I'_{t,k}} \leqslant \epsilon_k$$

and, since $\Delta\epsilon$ is an arbitrarily small quantity,

$$\frac{W'_{t,k} - W'_{t,k-1}}{I'_{t,k-1} - I'_{t,k}} = \epsilon_k \qquad (7)$$

It follows that $I'_{t,k}$, $W'_{t,k}$ may be represented by points forming a descending concave polygonal path. The slope of the segment $I'_{t,k}$, $W'_{t,k} \to I'_{t,k-1}$, $W'_{t,k-1}$ is equal (in absolute magnitude) to ϵ_k (see Fig. 30).

5. The ordinate of a point of the polygonal path defines the demand for the labour force W'_t corresponding to the aggregate capital investment I'_t which is minimum for the given W'_t. It may be assumed that the points of the polygonal path are fairly closely spaced. On the other hand, it may be assumed that the supply of labour (expressed in expenditure on constant wages) will follow demand on a limited scale. We shall therefore not be making a serious mistake if we assume that the supply of 'new' labour S_t equals the ordinate of one of the points F of the polygonal path (see Fig. 31).

It follows from (6) that the abscissa of this point $I_{t,F}$ is the lowest level of investment compatible with the growth of the labour force S_t at the growth rate r, the coefficient of scrapping a and the highest labour intensity of the production of the existing equipment x_t assigned for each branch. We will denote this level of aggregate capital investment by U_t (see Fig. 31).

128

The slope of the segment of the polygonal path beginning at the point F equals the magnitude of the parameter ϵ_F. This determines the choice of variants in individual branches. However, if the polygonal path is rigorously determined for the time t, a knowledge of ϵ_F is not essential for this purpose, since the variants corresponding to ϵ_F selected in the individual branches, i.e. the branch components of the quantities

$$I_{t,F} = U_t \quad \text{and} \quad W_{t,F} = S_t$$

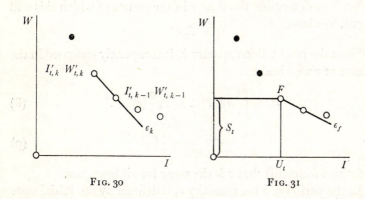

FIG. 30   FIG. 31

are directly known. However, if recourse is had to an approximate polygonal path, for example to one previously determined which is shifted downward in conformity with the general rise in labour productivity, ϵ_F is essential for the choice of variants in individual branches.

6. We have therefore concluded the first stage in our analysis in which the highest unit costs of labour, x_t in the operation of the existing fixed capital, are assumed to be given. We shall now demonstrate that, given certain further simplifications, x_t is determined throughout the period o, T by the initial state of the productive apparatus, by the rates of growth of production in the individual branches and by the branch coefficients of scrapping. Let us now assume that, as a result of technical progress: (i) the c_t' of the variants which are optimal in the period o, T is lower than the labour intensity of production using any equipment

existing at the time o; (ii) the c_t' of the variants of the period o, T is a decreasing function of time t. It is additionally assumed that (iii) the expression

$$\frac{1}{r} \cdot \frac{\ln (r+a)}{a}$$

is the same for all branches (this is the most far-reaching of the simplifications adopted).

It follows from (i) that equipment existing at the time o will be written off earlier than any items in the period o, T. It is not difficult to determine the time τ in the course of which this will occur. We have

$$P_t = P_0 e^{rt}$$

Since the production capacity P_0 is completely scrapped in the course of τ we obtain

$$P_0 = \int_0^\tau a P_0 e^{rt} dt = P_0 \frac{a}{r} (e^{r\tau} - 1) \tag{8}$$

or

$$\frac{r+a}{a} = e^{r\tau}; \quad \tau = \frac{1}{r} \ln \frac{r+a}{a} \tag{9}$$

It follows from (iii) that τ is the same for all branches.

In the period o, τ the quantity x_t is defined by the initial state of the basic capital, by the rates of growth of the given branch and by its coefficient of scrapping a. Consequently, during this period the polygonal path at the time t is defined by the coefficients r and a and by the different technical variants known at that time.

The position in the period τ, T is more complicated since x_t is here also dependent on the choice of variants in the period o, t. It is proved below on the basis of conditions (ii) and (iii) that the polygonal path at the time t is determined by the initial state of the equipment, by the coefficients r and a, by the dynamics of the growth of the labour force in the period o, t and by the technical variants at the time t.

It follows from (9) that

$$\frac{P_t}{P_{t-\tau}} = e^{r\tau} = \frac{r+a}{a}$$

or

$$a P_t = (r+a) P_{t-\tau} \tag{10}$$

Consequently, the production capacities scrapped in the interval t, $t+dt$, where $t > \tau$, are equal to the capacities of the equipment introduced in the interval $t-\tau$, $t-\tau+dt$. But, in accordance with condition (ii), the *actually* selected c'_t, which we denote by c''_t, are a decreasing function of t. Consequently, x_t is also a decreasing function of t in the period τ, T. It follows from this and from (10) that the equipment scrapped in the interval $t, t+dt$ is identical to that installed in the interval $t-\tau$, $t-\tau+dt$ and thus

$$x_t = c''_{t-\tau}; \quad a P_t x_t = (r+a) P_{t-\tau} c''_{t-\tau} \qquad (11)$$

Taking (1″) and (10) into consideration, we have

$$S_{t-\tau} = \Sigma \rho''_{t-\tau} P_{t-\tau} = \Sigma (r+a) P_{t-\tau} c''_{t-\tau}$$
$$- \Sigma a P_{t-\tau} x_{t-\tau} = \Sigma a P_t x_t - \Sigma a P_{t-\tau} x_t \qquad (12)$$

or
$$\Sigma a P_t x_t = S_{t-\tau} + \Sigma a P_{t-\tau} x_{t-\tau}$$

from which
$$W'_t = \Sigma \rho'_t P_t = \Sigma (r+a) P_t c'_t - \Sigma a P_t x_t$$
$$= \Sigma (r+a) P_t c'_t - (S_{t-\tau} + \Sigma a P_{t-\tau} x_{t-\tau})$$

It follows from this formula that, for $\tau \leqslant t < 2\tau$, the polygonal path I'_t, W'_t is determined by the coefficients r and a of all the branches, by the choice of variants in accordance with the criterion (4), by the increment of the labour force $S_{t-\tau}$ in the time $t-\tau$ and by the quantities $x_{t-\tau}$ for the individual branches. However, since $0 \leqslant t-\tau < \tau$, these quantities are determined by the initial state of the productive apparatus and by the coefficients r and a. It follows that the polygonal path and also its point U_t, S_t are fully determined at the time t by the coefficients r and a, by the variants existing at this time and by the aggregate flow of the labour force in the past.

It is now readily appreciable that this holds for any time t of the period 0, T: the polygonal path I'_t, W'_t and, consequently, also U_t, S_t will be dependent only on the stipulated factors, which also determine x_t.

It has therefore been proved that when conditions (i), (ii) and (iii) are satisfied the volume of investment determined by the method described in sections 3, 4 and 5 is minimum not only for a given state of the system at the time t, but simultaneously for all the t of the period o, T. The conditions from which it follows that the lifetime τ is the same for all branches are not as a rule satisfied (especially (iii)). Nevertheless, the proof of our theorem indicates that the minimum level of investment will probably be reached, even if approximately, throughout the entire plan period o, T.

7. Following the analysis of the problem as formulated, we must make some observations on the fixing of the coefficients of scrapping. One alternative is to maintain them at the level existing at the time o; another is to decide to introduce new branch coefficients a. In the latter case there will as a rule be a displacement of the polygonal path I'_0, W'_0 at the moment o and a corresponding alteration in the minimum of aggregate investment U_t.

Even if the 'new' level is not below the former level, this should not be taken as indicating that the 'reform' is necessarily desirable because an alteration of a may lead to the converse situation for some $t > 0$. In fact, this alteration affects the dynamics of the highest labour intensities of production with the old equipment. Corresponding to each set of branch coefficients of scrapping there is an approximately optimal time curve of investment in the period o, T arrived at by the methods outlined above. But in general these curves intersect, so that there need not necessarily be a curve lying lower than the others for all the t of the period o, T. A decision of the central planning organs is therefore needed whenever a discrepancy arises between the volume of capital investment and, consequently, of consumption in the short term and in the long term.

Another question arises in connection with coefficients of scrapping. It follows from section 3 that the choice of investment variants at the time t is based on criterion (4), in which ϵ is determined (in accordance with sections 4 and 5) by the polygonal path I'_t, W'_t and by the increment of the labour force at the moment t. It is clear that the 'durability' of equipment is not a factor which has any influence on such a process of the choice of investment variants. It should, however, be borne in mind that 'durability' is a problem which is closely connected with 'obsolescence' resulting from technical progress and that it is therefore an economic rather than a technical factor, to be decided by the central planning organs. If our approach to this problem is to adopt a fixed coefficient of scrapping for the given branch, a constant proportion of the production capacity characterized by the highest labour intensity is annually scrapped irrespective of whether or not it corresponds to the accepted definition of 'durability'.

To avoid misunderstanding, it should also be noted that expenditure on repairs, on spare parts and on other items which depreciate fairly rapidly is not regarded as capital investment connected with the scrapping of old equipment, but as running costs by analogy with expenditure on materials.

8. So far we have assumed that the only changes in the existing basic capital are in the scrapping of obsolete equipment in service. We shall now give general consideration to the problem of modernization in the sense of a reduction of labour costs in the various elements of a functioning productive apparatus as a result of investment which to some extent modifies this apparatus.

As has been noted in section 2 in the analysis of formula $(1')$, the object of replacement investment $a P_t i_t dt$ is to effect economies in live labour $a P_t (x_t - c_t) dt$. The ratio of these economies to the investment needed to effect them is $(x_t - c_t)/i_t$.

Let us assume that there is some scope for modernization of the productive apparatus of a given branch for which the ratio between the savings in live labour and the investment by means of which it is effected is greater than $(x_t - c_t)/i_t$. (It should be noted that $(x_t - c_t)/i_t$ is dependent on the variant i_t, c_t of new investment.)

In such a case it will be correct to substitute investment on modernization for all or a part of the 'replacement' investment (the amount of investment undertaken to reduce costs on live labour, and also the overall investment are unaffected). In fact, we shall then directly economize more on live labour than in the case of the scrapping and replacement of equipment with the highest unit expenditures on live labour x_t. In addition, we improve the scope for economy of live labour by the scrapping of obsolete equipment in the future.

In the given state of the fixed capital in service the scope for modernization is higher for those variants for which $(x_t - c_t)/i_t$ is lower. Consequently, in the given variant in which modernization is taken into account an increase in expenditure on live labour is no longer

$$\rho_t = rc_t - a(x_t - c_t) \tag{1'}$$

but is

$$\rho_t = rc_t - af_t\left(\frac{x_t - c_t}{i_t}\right) \tag{13}$$

where f_t is a decreasing function and

$$f_t((x_t - c_t)/i_t) \geqslant x_t - c_t$$

(the equality is omitted when there is no scope for appropriate modernization).

By analogy with (2) we shall now apply the term 'index of efficiency' to

$$E_t = i_t \frac{r + a}{r} + c_t - \frac{a}{r} f_t\left(\frac{x_t - c_t}{i_t}\right) \tag{14}$$

With an assigned ϵ the variant i_t/c_t is selected in accordance with the criterion $E_t = \min$, and if E_t is the same for two variants we once again select the least investment-intensive. The choice, in contrast to the deduction in section 3, will here be dependent on the value of $f_t((x_t - c_t)/i_t)$, which will differ for the different variants. Summing over the branches, we have

$$\Sigma E_t' r P_t dt \leqslant \Sigma E_t r P_t dt$$

where E_t' is an optimum variant. From this, reasoning in the same way as in section 3, we obtain

$$\epsilon I_t' + W_t' \leqslant \epsilon I_t + W_t$$

where

$$I_0' = \Sigma i_t'(r + a) P_t$$

as in section 3, but

$$W'_t = \Sigma rc'_t P_t - \Sigma af_t\left(\frac{x_t - c'_t}{i'_t}\right)$$

We may now draw the polygonal path I'_t, W'_t in the time t, which when taken in conjunction with the increase in labour force in this time S_t defines the minimum investment U_t. The level of investment will be less than or the same as when an economy of manpower is achieved solely by means of replacement investment.†

PART 2. ASSESSMENT OF DIFFERENT VARIANTS OF THE EXPENDITURE ON MATERIALS AND OF THE ROLE OF FOREIGN TRADE

1. So far we have assumed that the variants of investment in a given branch differ only in investment intensity i (in constant prices) and labour intensity c (in constant wages). When we come to consider the features of the different variants in relation to expenditure of materials, we have to calculate expenditure on materials in the investment variants which we compare and also in the items scrapped.

The complete capital investment and expenditure on live labour involved cannot be included in equations corresponding to (1) and (2), since they would then be taken into consideration twice or more times in the summing of these equations, because some of the branches produce materials for others. More detailed information concerning the plan is needed over a lengthy period o, T if this question is to be appropriately solved.

Since the plan is balanced from the point of view of expenditure of raw materials, certain rates of their expenditure in individual branches in the time t are accepted in it. When we select one of the investment variants we should give consideration to the positive or negative *deviations* from these rates. (As we

---

† A question which may arise is how to determine the coefficient of scrapping a for a given branch when there is modernization. This coefficient may readily be found by comparing the production with the new equipment $(r+a)P_t dt$ and the increase in the production of the branch $rP_t dt$, i.e. in the same way as in the complete replacement of obsolete equipment.

shall see, the same problem will arise in relation to expenditure on materials in items to be scrapped, where the total expenditure on live labour and materials per unit of production are highest. The expenditure of materials on these items may differ from the expenditures adopted in the plan, in which case it is once again necessary to take the *deviation* from the plan into consideration.)

We should now apparently proceed as follows. In addition to the capital investment and expenditure on live labour of the stage of production represented by the given branch, we must also consider the 'accompanying' capital investment and expenditure on live labour, corresponding to the expenditure of materials, but only on the scale of the deviation of this expenditure from the rates adopted in the plan. (For a variant in which the expenditure on intermediate and raw materials coincides with the amounts adopted in the plan we therefore have to consider only the capital investment and expenditure on live labour of the given phase.)

Such an approach would be correct only in the case of a closed economy. If we consider foreign trade, we shall arrive at different conclusions. A distinction may be drawn between 'currency' materials, i.e. those sold in foreign trade, and 'non-currency' materials, i.e. those not sold in this trade owing to high transportation costs (e.g. bricks) or because of other difficulties of sale (e.g. electric power and machine parts). In relation to 'non-currency' materials it is appropriate to use the method referred to above of allowing for the corresponding 'accompanying' capital investment and expenditure on live labour on the scale of deviations from the rates adopted in the plan. Such an approach is not as a rule satisfactory where 'currency' materials are concerned.

In fact, the plan for development of the economy includes a more or less definite plan of foreign trade, i.e we know the structure of exports and of the production aimed at reduction of imports. On the basis of this information we find a group of commodities for export or for 'import-substitution', for which the following condition is satisfied: if the currency cost of the 'currency' materials consumed is subtracted from the currency value of its production, and if the capital investment and labour for one currency rouble† of this net currency value are denoted by j and k respectively, the criterion for this commodity group for a given ϵ is expressed in the form $\epsilon j + k = \min$.

Further, if one investment variant is more economic than another with respect to expenditure on 'currency' materials by d currency roubles, the currency economized may be used to reduce the growth in the export or to increase the growth in the import of the commodity group referred to above and thereby to secure the maximum economy of 'calculated expenditure' for the given ϵ, namely on the scale $d(\epsilon j + k)$. (It should be noted that j and k should be selected from the technical point of view in relation to the criterion (4).)

2. It is now possible to compile formulae similar to (2) and (4) which allow for the scope of the different variants of the consumption of materials and for technical progress in this sphere. In the interests of simplicity we shall at present leave out of consideration expenditure of 'non-currency' materials (and also modernization).

Let us denote the currency value of the deviation of direct expenditure of materials from the quota in the time t by δ_t. In that case the 'calculated expenditure' on a unit of output will be

$$\epsilon i_t + c_t + \delta_t(\epsilon j_t + k_t)$$

The equipment which should be scrapped for a given ϵ is that for which the expression

$$x_t + \lambda_t(\epsilon j_t + k_t)$$

reaches a maximum, where x_t is the labour intensity of production for the scrapped equipment, and λ_t is the currency value of the deviation from the quota for the expenditure on materials for this output as adopted in the plan.

† [1 currency rouble = the amount of foreign currency equivalent to 1 rouble at the official exchange rate. *D.M.N.*]

Consequently, (2) will correspond to

$$E_t = [\epsilon i_t + c_t + \delta_t(\epsilon j_t + k_t)]\frac{r+a}{r} - [x_t + \lambda_t(\epsilon j_t + k_t)]\frac{a}{r} \quad (15)$$

or

$$E_t = \epsilon\left[i_t\frac{r+a}{r} + j_t\left(\delta_t\frac{r+a}{r} - \lambda_t\frac{a}{r}\right)\right]$$

$$- \left[(c_t + \delta_t k_t)\frac{r+a}{r} - (x_t + \lambda_t k_t)\frac{a}{r}\right] \quad (15')$$

where j_t and k_t are the same for all branches. As in the first part, the branch variants will be selected by the criterion $E_t = \min$, and once again should E_t be the same for two or more variants, the least capital-intensive is selected (the variant for which the first expression in the square brackets in formula (15') is least). Since r, a, f_t and k_t are the same for all variants of a given branch, and since this also holds with respect to λ_t for the given ϵ, we may write the criterion of the choice of variants at the time t in the form $\epsilon(i_t + \delta_t j_t) + (c_t + \delta_t k_t) = \min$.

If we denote the rate adopted in the plan for the currency value of materials expended per unit of output by n_t,

$$n_t + \delta_t = \sigma_t$$

will be the currency value of the total specific expenditure of materials in the given variant. Since n_t is the same for all variants, the criterion may be written for a given ϵ as

$$\epsilon(i_t + \sigma_t j_t) + (c_t + \sigma_t k_t) = \min \quad (16)$$

When two variants are equal, the one chosen is the one for which $i_t + \sigma_t j_t$ is less.

If we denote the optimum variants by i'_t, c'_t and δ'_t and the corresponding indices of efficiency by E'_t, we have $E'_t \leqslant E_t$.

Taking all branches together we obtain

$$\Sigma E'_t r P_t \delta_t \leqslant Er P_t \delta_t$$

and, by analogy with section 3 of the first part,

$$\epsilon I'_t + W'_t \leqslant \epsilon I_t + W_t,$$

where the capital investment and expenditure on live labour also allow for investment and expenditure which are a result of deviations in the consumption of raw materials from the rates adopted in the plan. I'_t and W'_t correspond to variants selected for a given ϵ by the criterion (16).

There is therefore a polygonal path I'_t, W'_t for the time t with the same properties as the polygonal path in Fig. 30. Taken in conjunction with the growth in manpower it determines the lowest level of capital investment U_t compatible with this growth. The most effective variants of individual branches are simultaneously determined.

3. Expenditure on 'non-currency' materials was left out of consideration in the last section in the interests of simplicity. We have previously noted that it is appropriate in relation to such materials to use the method of calculating the accompanying capital investment and expenditure on live labour in a given variant on a scale corresponding to the deviation between the expenditure on materials and the standards adopted in the initial plan. The highest expenditure on live labour and raw materials in an existing productive apparatus are determined as follows. When calculating expenditure on live labour and materials for a given ϵ, we consider, in addition to 'currency' materials, the capital investment and live labour corresponding to deviation from the plan of expenditure on 'non-currency' materials in the existing equipment. After this we determine which items of the total capacity aP_t should be scrapped in unit time on the basis of the total expenditure on live labour and materials in the given stage of production thus calculated.

However, we shall not complicate (15) and (16') by the inclusion of elements associated with different variants of the consumption of 'non-currency' materials, but shall assume that the investment associated with 'non-currency' materials in the variant under consideration or in the scrapped equipment is allowed for in i_t, and that the corresponding expenditure on live labour is allowed for in c_t. Hence the points of the polygonal path I'_t, W'_t show expenditure with allowance for expenditure on 'non-currency' materials on the scale of the deviation from the plan.

It may be assumed for the formula corresponding to the criterion (16) that i_t and c_t incorporate the *total* investment and expenditure on live labour connected with the expenditure of 'non-currency' raw materials. In order to avoid confusion between the values of i_t and c_t in the criterion as expressed in (16) and (15), we may replace these symbols in (16) in the new interpretation by r_t^* and c_t^*, and the expression then becomes

$$\epsilon(i_t^* + \sigma_t j_t) + (c_t^* + \sigma_t k_t) = \min \qquad (17)$$

4. In section 6, of part 1, where we left variants of the consumption of materials out of consideration in the problem, it was demonstrated that, given certain fairly considerable simplifications, the plan for the development of the economy (including coefficients of scrapping), taken in conjunction with the initial state of the basic capital and the dynamics of increase in manpower, fully defines the polygonal path I'_t, W'_t for the time t. We thus also determine the choice of variants at each moment of the period 0, T which minimizes capital investment I_t throughout this entire period. Because the conditions on which the proof of this theorem is based are not in general satisfied, it merely indicates the probability of the hypothesis to which it approximates.

In order to be able to prove this theorem, one further simplification must be introduced when calculating the different variants of the consumption of materials, namely that the highest labour intensity of production in the given branch x_t is characteristic of the items scrapped. (It follows from the two previous sections that this condition is not as a rule satisfied.) This simplification is, however, far less risky than the three 'special' premises of the proof of the theorem in section 6 of part 1 – in connection with the relatively small contribution of economy of materials to technical progress. To take progressive saving of raw materials into consideration does not therefore significantly reduce the probability that our theorem will be approximately suitable for practical purposes.

5. Now let us consider a completely different matter, namely the problem of an alteration of the originally planned branch structure of new production at a moment *t* as a result of optimum choice of variants in the manner described above. We have already demonstrated that minimization of investment may cause such changes in branch structure: the savings in investment outlays are used to increase consumption to such a degree that the growth in manpower is fully utilized.

This problem is even further complicated when variants of the consumption of materials are taken into consideration, since this causes simultaneous modification of the structure of the growth in foreign trade (in production both for export and for import-substitution).

In relation to foreign trade, the structure of the new production for export or for import-substitution has to be 'verified' on the basis of the parameter ϵ_t derived above. In fact, the choice of technological variants for a given commodity group does not differ fundamentally from the choice between production for export or for import-substitution of different commodity groups as a result of which one currency rouble is obtained. The value of $\epsilon_t i_t^*$ must therefore be compared for different commodity groups at the time *t*. Here i_t^* is the investment needed for the production in the given commodity group of the net currency worth of one currency rouble (i.e. after subtraction of the value of 'currency' materials). (Investment which serves for the production of 'currency' raw materials is consequently not taken into consideration in this capital investment.) The related expenditure on live labour for one currency rouble is denoted by c_t^*.

Comparison of the expressions $\epsilon_t i_t^* - c_t^*$ for different variants of production for export or for import-substitution with the new equipment does not lead to the choice of one or more commodity groups. The point is that the 'best' export variant has in general only fairly limited potential application in connection with the limited capacity of foreign markets. Nevertheless, comparison of these values will enable us to make some obvious corrections to the plan for the growth of foreign trade. This emerges as one further factor in the alteration of the structure of production.

The 'correct' level of investment, the 'new' consumption of raw materials and the 'new' structure of foreign trade for the time t are determined on the basis of the results of all these calculations. The greatest difficulties in plan reconstruction may arise from the 'correct' level of investment.

We have already mentioned that, for example, economy in investment may be used to increase consumption to such an extent that manpower continues to be fully used. In general, however, different branches produce investment and consumer goods. Let us assume that the 'correct' investment at the time 0, i.e. U_0, is considerably less than the production of finished investment goods for the internal market at the same time. This creates a difficult situation because an immediate shift in branch structure from investment to consumption is impossible.

The most rational approach will evidently be the following: the 'surplus' production of the capital goods-producing branches must be exported in exchange for consumer goods (over and above the 'normal' foreign trade). Although this exchange may possibly not be very advantageous, consumption will at all events increase. There will be a simultaneous rapid expansion in the production potential of consumer goods and no expansion in the potential for investment goods. The production of these goods will therefore correspond to U'_t within a comparatively short period t', and their 'excessive' export will cease to be necessary.

For $t > t'$ the difference between U_t and the production of investment goods is already of the order of dt and may be overcome in a short time.

The same applies to consumption of raw materials and to the structure of foreign trade for the whole period 0, T since the reference is here invariably to variants in the interval t, $t + dt$ (for example, to expenditure of coal or oil in *new* factories).

We thus arrive at a plan with new branch growth rates for the time t and therefore, by applying the foregoing methods to it, we in general arrive at a different polygonal path for this time. If it differs little from that originally established, we may regard our task of the choice of (technical and foreign trade) variants as completed. If not the process of gradual approximation will be continued.

This process will probably be convergent and even rapidly so, but there can be no absolute certainty of this. A warning should here be given against convergence arising from the lack in many instances of fundamentally differing technical variants (this is a basic problem relating to the practical use of the theory of invest- ment efficiency, which is a theory which cannot in itself *give rise* to new investment variants).

It should also be noted that in following the method described above we infringe the initial assumption that individual branches develop uniformly, although at different rates. It may readily be appreciated that this will not essentially modify the construction of the polygonal path I'_t, W'_t at the time t; at the same time the achievement of a minimum of investment through- out the entire period o, T becomes even more approximate.

6. We excluded modernization from consideration above. Let us return to (15) and introduce the notations

$$\left.\begin{aligned} h_t &= i_t + \delta_t j_t \\ b_t &= c_t + \delta_t k_t \\ v_t &= x_t + \lambda_t(\epsilon j_t + k_t) \end{aligned}\right\} \qquad (18)$$

We may now re-write (15) as

$$E_t = \epsilon h_t \frac{r+a}{r} + b_t - \frac{a}{r}(b_t - v_t)$$

If we then argue as in section 8 of the first part, taking the possibility of modernization into consideration, we obtain

$$E_t = \epsilon h_t \frac{r+a}{r} + b_t - \frac{a}{r} f_t\!\left(\frac{v_t - b_t}{h_t}\right)$$

Investment planning

where f_t is a decreasing function and

$$f_t[(v_t - b_t)/h_t] \geqslant v_t - b_t$$

For the given ϵ we select a variant by the criterion $E_t = \min$. It is now possible to construct the polygonal path I'_t, W'_t and to obtain for a given growth in manpower a value of U_t and branch variants which minimize aggregate investment at the time t.

PART III

THE MIXED ECONOMY

14. PROBLEMS OF FINANCING ECONOMIC DEVELOPMENT IN A MIXED ECONOMY

[1970]

1. The argument presented in this paper is based to a considerable extent on a distinction between two types of consumer goods: necessities and non-essentials. By necessities are meant goods which constitute a major part of the consumption of broad masses of the population. On the other hand non-essentials are consumed mainly by richer strata of the population. The chief items in necessities are staple foods.†

We make the following two assumptions on the financial aspects of economic development:

(*a*) There must be no inflationary price increases of necessities, in particular staple foods.

(*b*) No taxes should be levied on lower-income groups or necessities so that restraining of consumer demand must be effected through raising direct taxes on higher-income groups or indirect taxes on non-essentials.

It will be seen that these two assumptions are of considerable significance for the course of economic development because they make it dependent to a great extent on the rate of increase of the supply of necessities.

2. Let us now consider a development plan for a medium

---

† It follows from this definition that the list of necessities will widen with the long-run increase in the standard of living.

period, say, five to ten years. Let us denote the average rate of growth of the national income by r. We shall try to show that the rate of increase of the supply of necessities required in order to warrant the growth of the national income at a rate r without infringing upon our two basic postulates is a definite increasing function of r.

Let us assume for the moment that aggregate personal consumption increases proportionately to the national income, i.e., at a rate r, and that there are no major changes in the distribution of personal incomes between various classes of the population, such as, e.g., those caused by the increase in the prices of necessities or by changes in taxation. Then to the rate of growth of the national income r there corresponds a definite rate of increase of demand for necessities c_n. If the rate of growth of national income and thus of total consumption r is equal to the rate of increase of population q, so that per capita consumption remains unaltered, the rate of increase of demand for necessities is equal to q as well: $r = q = c_n$. If, however, the rate of growth r is higher than the rate of increase of population q then per capita consumption will increase (approximately) at a rate $r - q$ and the rate of increase of per capita demand for necessities will be $c_n - q$ which will in general be lower than $r - q$. If we denote the average income elasticity of demand for necessities by e we can say that

$$c_n - q = e(r - q)$$

where e is in general less than one. From this we derive

$$c_n = q + e(r - q)$$

The average income elasticity of demand for necessities e depends on such elasticities for various classes of the population and on income distribution between these classes.

We also should take into consideration that, strictly speaking, e changes within the period considered. Indeed, as per capita consumption increases the income elasticity of demand for necessities tends to decline. This effect is the more pronounced the higher the rate of growth r, so that e should be really assumed a declining function of r. But as r is in fact a rather low percentage and the period encompassed not very long the influence of r upon e is of no great importance and may be neglected.

Thus e in the above equation may be considered a constant so that c_n appears to be a linear function of r. This is shown diagrammatically in Fig. 32. The straight line inclined less than 45° ($e < 1$) passes through the point B for which both the abscissa

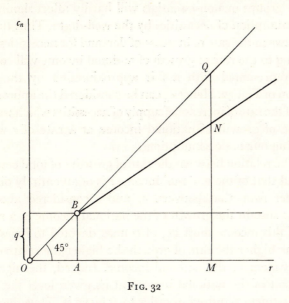

FIG. 32

and the ordinate are equal to the rate of increase in population q. This point stands for the situation where there is no increase in total per capita consumption and thus the demand for necessities increases at a rate q as well. If $r = OM$ is higher than q, then the same is true of $c_n = MN$; however, c_n is less than r, the point N being situated below the 45° line OQ.

3. We assumed in the preceding paragraph that total consumption changes proportionately to the national income. This, however, was intended merely to simplify a stage in our argument. In fact it may be necessary, as will be seen below, to restrain consumption in order to allow for a more rapid increase

in investment than that of national income. In such a case consumption will have to be restrained by taxation. According to our rules of the game this will consist of raising taxes on higher-income groups and on non-essentials. The question arises here whether this will not upset the functional relations between c_n and r arrived at above.

It should be noted, however, that the taxation of higher-income groups or non-essentials will hardly affect significantly the consumption of necessities by the well-do-to. Thus the relation between the rate of increase of demand for necessities corresponding to the rate of growth of national income will continue to be represented with a fair approximation by the above equation or Fig. 32. Hence c_n can be considered the approximate value of the rate of increase of supply of necessities which warrants the rate of growth of national income at a rate of r without infringing our basic assumptions.

4. The relation between the rate of growth c of total consumption and that of the national income r is of an entirely different character from that between c_n and r considered above. In order to sustain the growth of the national income at a rate r a part of this income must be, of course, devoted to investment. Now the higher the rate of growth the higher the relative share of investment in the national income. Indeed, the higher the increment of the national income at its given level the higher the investment required in order to achieve it. Thus the higher the ratio of the increment of the national income to its level – or the higher the rate of growth – the higher the ratio of investment to the national income.

Imagine that we start from a position characterized by a rate of growth, r_0, to which corresponds a certain relative share of investment in the national income. If this rate of growth is continued the relative share of investment in the national income is maintained (unless, of course, there is a change in the capital–output ratio). But if the average rate of growth envisaged in the plan is higher so will be the average relative share of investment in the national income. This means that the relative share of investment in the national income will be increasing from the beginning to the end of the plan. (For instance, it may be 14 per cent at the beginning of a five-year plan, 20 per cent at its end, and 17 per cent on the average.) The relative share in consumption in the national income will be correspondingly falling. In other words the average rate of growth of consumption c will be

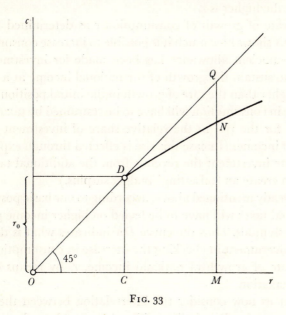

FIG. 33

lower than that of the national income r. The difference, $r - c$, will be the higher the greater is the average rate of growth of the national income r in relation to r_0; because where r is higher the acceleration of the rate of growth as compared with the initial position will be greater and thus the increase in the relative share of investment in the national income will be greater in the period considered.

The relation between c and r is represented on Fig. 33 by the curve DN. The point D represents the initial position at which the rate of growth equals $r_0 = OC$. If this is the rate adopted in the plan consumption need not increase more slowly than the national income; i.e. $c = CD = r_0$. Thus the point D is situated on a 45° line OQ.

If, however, the average rate of growth of the national income $r = OM$ envisaged in the plan is higher than r_0 the rate of growth of consumption $c = MN$ is lower than r and thus is below the 45° line OQ, the difference $r - c = NQ$ being more marked the higher is r.

The rate of growth of consumption c as determined by the curve DN shows how much it is possible to increase consumption after a sufficient allowance has been made for investment required to sustain the growth of the national income at a rate r, If r is higher than the rate of growth in the initial position r_0, the increase in consumption will have to be restrained by taxation to provide for the rise in the relative share of investment in the national income. (In case this rise is effected through expansion of private investment the revenue from the additional taxation serves to create an 'offsetting' budget surplus.)

As already mentioned above, according to our basic postulates additional taxes will have to be levied on higher income groups or non-essentials. Thus the curve DN indicates what is the task of the government in checking the increase in consumption at a given rate of growth of national income, r, by means of this type of taxation.

5. Let us now consider the interrelation between the three rates, c_n, r and c. We shall consider the case where the capital–output ratio does not increase over the level at the initial position; however, all our subsequent argument applies fully also to the case where such an increase does take place.

Let us combine Figs. 32 and 33 in Fig. 34. It will be noticed that $r_0 = O'C'$ is greater than $q = OA$. Thus the rate of growth of national income in the initial position is assumed here to be higher than the rate of increase of population.

It is clear that of the three rates of growth in question c_n, c, r our diagram determines two if one is given. Now in underdeveloped mixed economies it is c_n, the rate of increase of supply of necessities, that can be considered as given. The increase in produc-

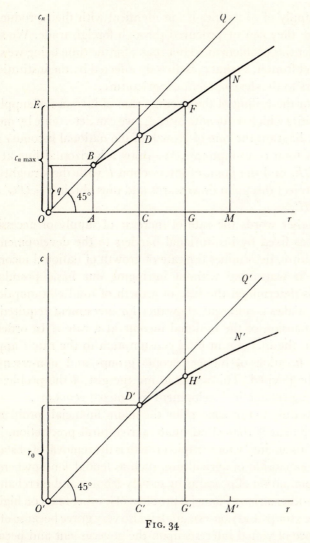

FIG. 34

tion of necessities, especially of staple food, is limited by institutional factors, such as feudal land ownership and domination of peasants by merchants and money-lenders. As a result c_n the average rate of increase in the supply of necessities over the planning period, is kept down to a rather low level. It is true that supply of necessities is not identical with their production because they can be procured through foreign trade. We shall consider this problem at a later stage; for the time being we shall abstract from it, so that c_n is directly affected by the institutional barriers to the development of agriculture.

From the ceiling of the average rate of increase of supply of necessities which we denote by $c_{n\,max}$ we can determine by means of our diagram the rate of growth of the national income r and that of total consumption c. We draw a horizontal line at the level OE, find the point of intersection F with the straight line BN, project this point downwards and thus obtain $r = O'G'$ and $c = G'H'$.

In other words the rate of increase of supply of necessities $c_{n\,max}$, as fixed by institutional barriers to the development of agriculture, determines the rate of growth of national income r which is warranted without infringing our basic postulates. Next is determined the rate of growth of total consumption c which makes a sufficient allowance for investment required for the expansion of the national income at a rate r. In order to restrain the increase in total consumption to the rate c appropriate taxation of higher income groups and non-essentials must be devised. This seems to me the gist of the problem of financing economic development in a mixed economy.

According to this conception the main 'financial' problem of development is that of adequate agricultural production. The key to 'financing' a more rapid growth is the removal of obstacles to the expansion of agriculture, such as feudal land-ownership and domination of peasants by money-lenders and merchants.

The other strictly financial problem of levying taxes on higher-income groups and non-essentials is also very grave because of the influence of vested interests upon the government and because of the difficulty of overcoming tax evasion. However, the main bottleneck in the balanced growth of a mixed economy seems usually to be the low rate of expansion of agriculture resulting from agrarian conditions. Indeed, the rate of growth of the national income determined by it in the way described above will not usually be so high as to present an insuperable problem of financing investment by taxation in such a way as not to affect low-income groups or the prices of necessities. However, if the problem of the inadequate increase of agricultural production were solved by means of agrarian reform, etc., so as to warrant a higher rate of balanced growth, a parallel effort would have to be made in the fiscal sphere in order to achieve an increase in taxation of high-income groups and non-essentials.

6. What happens, however, if the rate of growth of national income exceeds the level warranted by the rate of increase of supply of necessities? Let us assume that $r = OM$ is higher than OG (see Fig. 34). Then c_n equals MN instead of GF. As the supplies of necessities forthcoming are inadequate to meet demand their prices rise.

Equilibrium is restored through a fall in the real income of the broad masses of the population while the extra profits of the capitalists do not increase the demand for necessities since they are spent on non-essentials or accumulated. Such extra accumulation reduces the need for taxation in order to finance investment. This is a reflection of the fact that the consumption of necessities and thus total consumption is restrained by the increase in their prices. It is true that this is partly offset by the extra consumption of non-essentials; but to the extent to which extra profits are accumulated, total consumption is on balance restrained.

Thus this type of growth involving inflationary price increases of necessities – against the first of our basic postulates – is definitely to the advantage of the upper classes. A relatively high rate of growth is secured without resorting to a radical reform of the agrarian conditions and with lower taxation of these classes than would be necessary if growth at this rate were balanced.

The aggregate consumption of the broad masses of the population is the same as it would be if the growth of national income were at a rate warranted by the actual rate of increase in the supply of necessities, i.e. it is the same at a rate of growth OM as at a rate of growth OG; employment is higher when $r = OM$, but real wages are correspondingly lower as a result of the increase in the prices of necessities. The higher relative share of investment which is necessary to increase the rate of growth from OG to OM is achieved at least in part at the expense of this fall in real wages.

Imagine that the planned rate of growth of the national income is OM. Allowing for the investment necessary to implement that plan the planned rate of increase in consumption is $M'N'$. This plan will be fulfilled but the rate of increase in supply of necessities will be GF and not MN and the rate of increase in the consumption of non-essentials will accordingly be higher. A corresponding shift will occur in the structure of investment: the development of industries producing luxury goods will be emphasized. The rate of growth will indeed be higher than OG but growth itself will be lopsided.

7. We have so far disregarded foreign trade. However, for some countries it is a serious omission because they are able to purchase necessities abroad in exchange for exports, especially in the case where they are endowed with rich natural resources (e.g. the oil-producing countries). We shall try now, therefore, to introduce foreign trade into our model.

The rate of increase of supply of necessities c_n stood for the rate of production of necessities when foreign trade was disregarded and it was on this assumption that the argument in section 6 was based. If we introduce foreign trade, however, the straight line BN in Fig. 34 ceases to represent the rate of increase of *production* of necessities p_n. If imports of necessities can be increased, more rapidly than their home production, the rate of increase of the latter is lower than that of the total supply of necessities.

Imagine that such is the case where $r = r_0$; i.e. where the rate of growth of the national income adopted in the plan is equal to the rate of growth in the initial position. Then where

$$r = r_0 = OC$$

the curve IP (see Fig. 35) relating the rate of increase in *home production* of necessities, p_n, to the rate of growth of national income, r, which it can warrant without infringing our basic postulates, will be situated below the straight line BN (which shows the rate of increase in the supply of necessities which is needed at different growth rates). The gap between BN and IP is made good through foreign trade.

However, as r becomes higher than r_0, the difference $c_n - p_n$ between the ordinates of the curves BN and IP will become smaller. Indeed, the higher the rate of growth, r, the more rapidly will the demand for imports other than necessities rise, and in particular the demand for investment goods. In general it will be increasingly difficult to balance imports by a rise in exports because of certain limitations either of supplies of export goods or of foreign markets. Thus it will become increasingly difficult to increase imports of necessities at a rate which permits the increase in their domestic production to lag behind demand requirements. Finally at the rate of growth corresponding to the point of intersection of the curves BN and IP home production and imports of necessities rise *pari passu*, c_n being equal to p_n. If the rate of growth of national income is pushed beyond that point, it appears that, in order to provide adequate imports of items other than necessities the rate of growth of the domestic production of necessities would have to be higher than that of the required supply.

Fig. 35 shows the influence of foreign trade upon the rate of balanced growth. Let us draw, as in Fig. 34, a horizontal line at the level OE of the maximum rate of growth of production of necessities $p_{n\,max}$. (We denoted this rate $c_{n\,max}$ in section 5 because $c_{n\,max} = p_{n\,max}$ if there is no foreign trade.) But now it will be the point of intersection of this line with the curve IP rather than with the curve BN that determines the rate of balanced growth. This rate of growth of the national income OK is higher than OG that would prevail without the contribution of foreign trade to the acceleration of the increase in the supply of necessities. Such will be, for instance, the position in the oil-producing countries.

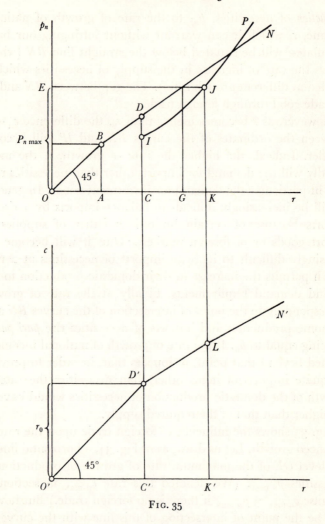

FIG. 35

If, however, the foreign trade situation is less favourable, so that the difference $c_n - p_n$ at the lower ranges of r is smaller than in Fig. 35, the contribution of foreign trade to the achievement of a higher rate of balanced growth may be nil (see Fig. 36). The horizontal line at the level OE here passes through the point of intersection of the curve IP with the straight line BN.

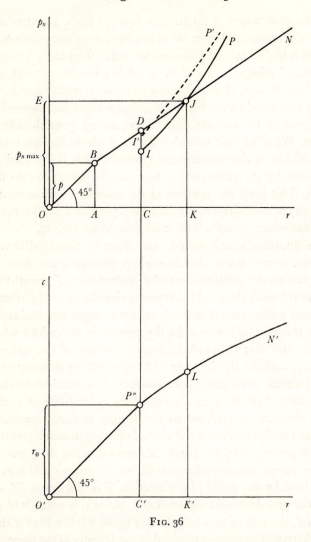

FIG. 36

Indeed, the position may even be reversed. Foreign trade may affect the rate of balanced growth adversely by aggravating rather than relieving the problem of the adequate increase of the supply of necessities. Such will be, for instance, the case if the relation between p_n and r is represented by the dotted curve $I'P'$,

In the case where a favourable foreign trade position may permit a given rate of increase of production of necessities p_n to warrant a higher rate of balanced growth r the purely financial problem of adequate taxation of higher-income groups and non-essentials will, of course, grow in relative importance.

8. We assumed tacitly in the preceding section that imports are fully covered by exports thus disregarding possible capital imports. We shall now consider the case where foreign credits are available to the government concerned for the period encompassed by the plan (which was not the case prior to that period). This eases the position of the economy with regard to the supply of necessities and thus makes possible a higher rate of non-inflationary growth. This is illustrated by Fig. 37.

As a situation which would exist if no foreign credits were forthcoming we choose the case where foreign trade does not contribute to the achievement of a higher rate of growth; the horizontal line at the level OE representing the rate of increase in the actual production of necessities; the straight line BN representing the rate of increase in the supply of necessities which warrants the rate of non-inflationary growth of the national income r; and finally the curve IP representing the respective rate of increase of required home-produced necessities – all three intersecting at point J. As a result of the availability of foreign credits the rate of increase in the supply of home produced necessities which warrants the rate of non-inflationary growth r will be represented by the curve SZ situated below the curve IP. In consequence the rate of non-inflationary growth will now be determined by the point of intersection T of the curve SZ and the horizontal drawn at the level OE. Since this point is to the right of J, the rate of non-inflationary growth OU is higher than OK which could have been realized in the absence of the import of capital.

It will be seen that, if there were no foreign credits, the rate of growth OU would require a rate of increase in the supply of necessities UV higher than UT and a still higher rate of increase in the *production* of necessities UW in order to cover the gap in

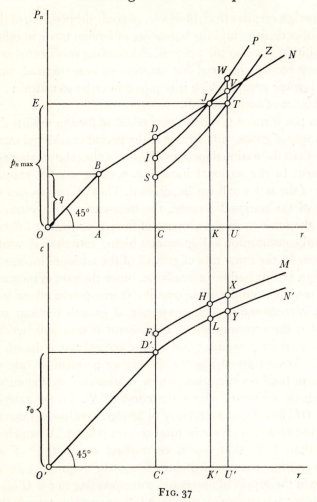

FIG. 37

foreign trade in other commodities. Foreign credits make it possible to reduce the rate of increase in the production of necessities for internal consumption to UT and to cover the gap in foreign trade in other commodities reflected in the discrepancy WV. Thus foreign credits will be used not only to supplement the home supplies of necessities but to make possible the required higher imports of other goods such as machinery or raw materials.

The mixed economy

9. Foreign credits affect, however, not only the problem of the supply of necessities and the balancing of foreign trade in other commodities, but also the problem of financing investment and thus they reduce the need for taxation of non-essentials and higher income groups which is required in order to restrain the consumption of non-essentials.

Or to put it more precisely: as a result of foreign credits the total supply of goods will increase in the period considered more rapidly than the national income. However, the relative share of investment in the national income depending on the rate of growth of the latter will not be affected. Thus at a given rate of growth of the national income, the time-curve of investment will be the same as in the absence of foreign credits. It follows that total consumption will grow at a higher rate than it would have done at the same rate of growth of the national income if no foreign credits had been available. Since the rate of increase in the required supply of necessities (home-produced or imported) corresponding to a given rate of growth remains the same, it is the consumption of non-essentials that will benefit and the need for restraining this will be accordingly reduced.

In the lower part of Fig. 32 the higher permissible rate of increase in total consumption is now represented by the curve $F'M'$ which is situated above the curve $D'N'$. To the rate of growth OU based on availability of foreign credits thus corresponds the rate of increase in total consumption $U'X'$ which is higher than $U'Y'$ that would correspond to $r = O'U'$ if no foreign credits were forthcoming. Since the required rate of increase in the supply of necessities corresponding to $r = O'U'$ is UV with or without foreign credits, it is the rate of increase in the consumption of non-essentials that will benefit from $U'X'$ being higher than $U'Y'$.

10. It will be seen that, when the import of capital is used to raise the rate of non-inflationary growth by supplementing the home supplies of necessities, the reduction of the taxes required to finance investment appears merely as a by-product of the process involved. However, it is perfectly feasible that capital

imports may be used solely for budgetary purposes. The rate of non-inflationary growth remains at the level OK while taxation of non-essentials and higher incomes is reduced. As a result the rate of increase of total consumption is $K'H'$ and not $K'L'$, the consumption of non-essentials rising correspondingly faster. If the increased demand is directed towards foreign non-essentials it is reflected in their imports. In the case where home-produced non-essentials are the object of this demand the production of investment goods has to be kept down by the authorities if inflationary pressures on necessities are to be avoided and thus investment requirements have to be to this extent satisfied by imports. In either case foreign credits are directly or indirectly wasted on non-essentials while economic growth is not accelerated, although in the second case foreign credits seem to be used 'productively'.

It should be noticed that even in the case where foreign credits *are* used to raise the rate of growth of the national income it is by no means *necessary* to reduce the taxation of non-essentials and higher incomes which permits a relatively faster increase in the consumption of non-essentials in the period encompassed by the plan. Indeed, the relief in the financing of investment which is a by-product of capital imports may be used for an expansion of government expenditure for such purposes as low-cost housing, health and education.

At this point the question may arise how it is that capital imports manage to benefit the country considered in two ways. This, however, follows clearly from the two functions that capital imports perform: first, the availability of a certain amount of foreign exchange enables the country concerned to modify its *structure* of home supplies, e.g. to increase the supply of necessities; second, by raising the *volume* of home supplies without creating new incomes foreign credits contribute to the economic surplus and thus they reduce *pro tanto* the need for domestic savings.

15. SOCIAL AND ECONOMIC ASPECTS OF 'INTERMEDIATE REGIMES'
[1967]

1. History has shown that lower-middle-class and rich peasantry are rather unlikely to perform the rôle of the ruling class. Whenever social upheavals have enabled representatives of these classes to rise to power, they have invariably served the interests of big business (often allied with the remnants of the feudal system). This despite the fact that there is a basic contradiction between the interests of the lower-middle-class and big business, to mention only the displacement of small firms by business concerns.

Are there any specific conditions today favouring the emergence of governments representing the interests of the lower-middle-class (including in this also the corresponding strata of the peasantry)? It would seem that such conditions do arise at present in many underdeveloped countries:

(i) At the time of achieving independence the lower-middle-class is very numerous while big business is predominantly foreign-controlled with a rather small participation of native capitalists.

(ii) Patterns of government economic activities are now widespread. Apart from the obvious case of socialist countries, state economic interventionism plays an important rôle in developed capitalist countries.

(iii) It is possible to obtain foreign capital also through credits granted by socialist countries.

2. In the process of political emancipation – especially if this is not accompanied by armed struggle – representatives of the lower-middle-class rise in a way naturally to power.

To keep in power they must:

(a) achieve not only political but also economic emancipation, i.e. gain a measure of independence from foreign capital;

(*b*) carry out a land reform;

(*c*) assure continuous economic growth; this last point is closely connected with the other two.

By endeavouring at least to limit foreign influence, the lower-middle-class government heads into conflict with the 'comprador' elements. When carrying out land reform it clashes with the feudal landlords. However, it may not necessarily be inclined to defy the native upper-middle-class. Reliance on this class in the strategy of economic development could easily result in the repetition of a well-known historical pattern – the final submission of the lower-middle-class to the interests of big business.

This, however, is prevented by the weakness of the native upper-middle-class and its inability to perform the rôle of 'dynamic entrepreneurs' on a large scale. The basic investment for economic development must therefore be carried out by the state which leads directly to the pattern of amalgamation of the interests of the lower-middle-class with state capitalism.

The realization of this pattern is facilitated by the participation of the state in the management of the economy, a phenomenon characteristic of our era. A large part of the world population today lives in the centrally-planned socialist economies. But also in the developed capitalist countries there prevails today a fair measure of state interventionism which at the very least is aimed at preventing the business downswings. We are all 'planners' today, although very different in character. No wonder, then, that the underdeveloped countries, striving to expand their economic potential as fast as possible (while the main concern of the developed capitalist countries is to utilize fully the available productive capacities), tend to draw up plans of economic development. The next step is to provide for a large volume of investment in the public sector, since, as shown by experience, the private initiative cannot be relied upon to undertake an adequate volume of investment of appropriate structure. Thus state capitalism is closely connected with planning of one form or another which underdeveloped countries can hardly avoid today.

Evolution in this direction could be counteracted significantly by the pressure of the imperialist countries, exerted by attaching appropriate 'strings' to credits granted. Since underdeveloped countries cannot do without some inflow of foreign capital, pressure of this kind could be highly effective in changing the lower-middle-class governments into servile tools of big business allied with the feudal class. Apart from an 'ideological' victory, imperialist countries would gain a better foothold for defending their 'old' investments in underdeveloped countries and for a 'new' expansion in this sphere. A significant obstacle to these imperialist pressures, though, is the possibility of obtaining credits from socialist countries. Its effect is reflected not merely in the amount of capital actually received by underdeveloped countries from this source, but also in strengthening their bargaining position in dealing with the financial-capitalist powers. The competition with the socialist countries for influence in the 'intermediate regimes' forces those powers to grant credits without attaching conditions as to the internal economic policy, although the imperialist governments do try to obtain as much as possible in this respect.

3. The social system in which the lower-middle-class co-operates with state capitalism calls for a somewhat more detailed discussion. To be sure, this system is highly advantageous to the lower-middle-class and the rich peasants; state capitalism concentrates investment on the expansion of the productive potential of the country. There is thus no danger of forcing the small firms out of business, which is a characteristic feature of the early stage of industrialization under *laissez faire*. Next, the rapid development of state enterprises creates executive and technical openings for ambitious young men of the numerous ruling class. Finally, the land reform, which is not preceded by an agrarian revolution, is conducted in such a way that the middle-class which directly exploits the poor peasants – i.e. the money-lenders and merchants – maintains its position, while the rich peasantry achieves considerable gains in the process.

The antagonists of the ruling class are: from above, the upper-middle-class allied with foreign capital and the feudal land-owners; from below, the small land-holders and landless peasants, as well as the poor urban population – workers in small factories and unemployed or casually employed, mainly migrants from the countryside in search of a source of livelihood. On the other hand, white-collar workers and the not very numerous workers of large establishments – who in underdeveloped countries are in a privileged position as compared with the urban and rural paupers – are frequently, especially when employed in state enterprises, allies of the lower-middle-class rather than its antagonists.

4. As to the antagonistic 'higher' classes, the feudals are generally deprived of political significance by the land reform. They might retain parts of their land through fictitious sales to relatives (so as to evade the ceiling) but this does not put them in a strong position in the political and social life of the country. On the other hand, the relation to the upper-middle-class may range from far-reaching nationalization (usually with compensation) to a mere limitation of the scope of private investment coupled with attempts, as a rule rather ineffective, to adjust its structure to the general goals of development.

The political importance of big business in the country corresponds to these variants. In any case its tendency to oppose the government is checked by the fear of the urban and rural proletariat, from which it is effectively separated by the ruling lower-middle-class. The choice of the particular variant of dealing with big business is determined not so much by the ideology of the ruling class, as by the strength of the former. Without taking into consideration the existing economic conditions, one might expect more 'socialism' from a Nehru than from a Nasser. It was, however, the other way round, because at the time of gaining political independence, big business in India was much stronger than in Egypt.

5. Potentially at least, the urban and rural paupers are antagonistic towards the ruling class since they do not benefit from the change of social system such as described above, and

profit relatively little from economic development. The land reform is conducted in such a way that a major share of the land available goes to the rich and medium-rich peasants while the small land-holders and the rural proletariat receive only very little land. Insufficient effort is made to free the poor peasantry from the clutches of money-lenders and merchants and to raise the wages of farm labourers. The resulting agrarian situation is one of the factors limiting agricultural output within the general economic development, as under the prevailing agrarian relations the small farms are unable to expand their production. The same is true of larger farms cultivated by tenants. The lagging of agriculture behind general economic growth leads to an inadequate supply of foodstuffs and an increase in their prices, which is again to the disadvantage of the 'stepsons' of the system. Even if the aggregate real incomes of those strata do not decline as a result of the increase in employment, they do not show any appreciable growth.

Though the poorest strata of the society have thus no reason to be happy, they do not, for the time being at least, constitute a danger for the present system. The poor peasantry and rural proletariat are controlled by some form of a local oligarchy comprised of the petty bourgeoisie (merchants and money-lenders), the richer peasants and smaller landlords. The urban population without stable employment and even home workers and workers in small factories are not too dangerous either, because they are permanently threatened by unemployment and are difficult to organize.

In this contact one can easily understand the repressions against the communists observable in a number of 'intermediate regimes'. This is not a question of competition between parallel ideologies; the communists are simply at least potential spokesmen for the rural and urban paupers, and the lower-middle-class is quite rightly afraid of the political activization of the latter.

It is true that this lower-middle-class and the prosperous peasants are not really rich; in many instances their standard of living is lower than that of workers in developed countries. But in comparison to the masses of poor peasants, who also flood the cities as unemployed or badly-paid home workers, the petty bourgeois is a tycoon with a lot to lose. In this context it is no coincidence either that the governments in question favour religion – even to the point of adopting an official religion – and show a tendency towards external expansion and militarism associated with it.

6. On the international scene, the internal position of the ruling lower-middle-class finds its counterpart in the policy of neutrality between the two blocs: an alliance with any of the blocs would strengthen the corresponding antagonist at home. At the same time this neutrality is very important in the context of foreign credits mentioned above.

The 'intermediate regimes' are the proverbial clever calves that suck two cows: each block gives them financial aid competing with the other. Thus has been made possible the 'miracle' of getting out of the United States some credits with no strings attached as to the internal economic policy.

It should be still noticed that foreign credits are of great importance to the 'intermediate regimes'. The lagging of their agriculture behind their overall development – caused to a great extent by institutional factors – results in a shortage of foodstuffs which the state covers partly by imports (since the paupers must not be pushed to the extremes). This creates additional difficulties in the already strained balance of payments for which the remedy is sought in foreign credits.

Such a position in international relations defends the 'intermediate regimes', as said above, against the pressure from imperialist powers aimed at restoration of the 'normal' rule of big business in which the foreign capital would play an appreciable rôle (though more limited than in the past). Without such external pressures it is highly unlikely that the amalgamation of lower-middle-class with state capitalism would be destroyed and the classical capitalism reinstated.

The above was published in Poland at the end of 1964. Although

167

Indonesia did not contradict at that time the pattern of 'intermediate regimes' we outlined, it was by no means its representative example and this for the following reasons:

(*a*) In economic policy Indonesia lagged considerably behind a typical 'intermediate regime'. The agrarian reform was in actual fact fairly ineffective and changed relatively little in Indonesian agrarian conditions. Nor did the government make any consistent effort in terms of industrialization and planning; in particular a violent inflation was permitted to develop. More than that, the government made a point of granting priority to the 'national integration' (inclusive of the claims to West Irian and the Northern Borneo) over economic and social problems.

(*b*) On the other side, the foreign policy of Indonesia was more anti-imperialist and anti-colonialist than that of other 'intermediate regimes'. This radicalism was partly associated with the territorial claims mentioned above (in particular with 'confrontation with Malaysia') but was definitely general in character.

(*c*) The by-product of the fight for incorporation of West Irian and of the 'confrontation with Malaysia' was the expansion of the army – which, i.a. imposed a considerable burden on the economy – and the enhancing of the political power of its higher echelons.

(*d*) As contrasted with other 'intermediate regimes', Indonesia had a very large communist party. It was rooted mainly in the dissatisfaction of the poor peasants and farm labourers. However, it co-operated with the regime on the basis of support for its anti-imperialist policies without militating strongly against its neglect of domestic economic and social problems and not being prepared for a showdown with reactionary middle-classes associated closely with the army. It is obvious that the communist party represented here a much greater threat to these classes than in other 'intermediate regimes' which, however, was still potential rather than actual.

It is the situation outlined above that created the basis for subsequent developments in Indonesia. The full history of the events of 30 September 1965 has not yet been written. So much is clear, that the communists did not attempt a takeover and that in fact these events played the rôle of *Reichstagsfeuer*. The anti-communist terror that followed was unprecedented even in the history of counter-revolutions: in the space of a few months about 400,000 people were murdered. The higher echelons of the army representing largely the reactionary middle-class and rich peasants or even semi-feudal elements thus eliminated the 'anomaly' of a powerful communist party in an intermediate regime.

Also the foreign policy swung back to 'normal'. Although as said above, the army derived a great measure of their power from the policy of 'confrontation with Malaysia' it is just they who have now terminated this policy. In general the radicalism of Indonesian foreign policy is over, although, at least for the time being, the non-alignment policy has not been abolished.

The economic problems which are emphasized by the new government are being blamed on their predecessors. However, the conclusions drawn from the catastrophic economic situation do not point at all to more planning or agrarian reform. The terror that rages not only against communists but radicals in general is probably considered an adequate substitute for progressive economic and social policies.

INDEX

accumulation, *see* productive accumulation

administrative services, 2, 3

agriculture, 44

  in underdeveloped countries, 152, 166, 167

balance of payments, 122, 167

balance of trade, 4, 8, 16

big business, in underdeveloped countries, 162, 165

bottlenecks, 11n, 50, 122

building sites, limit to possible number of, 44

buildings, services rendered by, 2, 3, 4

capital

  extra profits of, when growth rate exceeds rate of increase of supply of necessities, 153

  'freezing' of, in excessive number of building sites, 44

  outlay of, per unit of increment in national income, 46

capital charges, shadow and actual, 113n

capital equipment (fixed capital), 1, 4

  degree of utilization of, 11, 12, 18–19, 20

  durability of, 132–3

  investment equals volume of, delivered in given year, 10, 34n

  life span of, 2, 17, 28n, 61; assumed equal for all types of equipment in concept of production curve, 112; increasing growth rate by shortening, 77–82; increasing labour productivity by shortening, 58–60; optimum, without sacrifice of consumption, 82–4

  in process of construction, 4, 14, 34n

  rate of increase of, at constant growth rate, 17–18, 21

ratio of output to, *see* capital–output ratio

recasting, rejuvenation, transformation of, *see under those headings*

relation between national income and stock of, 18–20, 21n

scrapping of obsolete, *see* scrapping

capital goods

  capital intensity of consumer goods and of, 14

  export of surplus, in exchange for consumer goods, 142

capital intensity of production

  availability of labour in choice of, 99

  case in which it is advantageous to reduce 70, 95–8

  of capital and consumer goods, 14

  effect of shift towards higher, on labour productivity with different types of technical progress, 54, 55, 64

  in manufacturing and primary production, 122–3

  optimum, without sacrifice of consumption, 82–4

  relative increase in rate of productive accumulation and in, 87

  standard of living during 'recasting' as key problem in choice of, 69

capital–output ratio, 10, 53

  choice of (with unlimited labour), 85–101

  depends on structure of investment, 14

  increasing growth rate by raising, 61–76

  in investment sector, 103–4

  and labour productivity, 13, 35; acceleration of increase in labour productivity by raising, 56–8

  for total capital, 15

coal mines, long construction-period for, 44

171

Index

communists, in underdeveloped countries, 166, 168–9

construction
  capital in process of, in calculating national income, 4, 14, 34n
  period required for, 34n, 44

consumer goods
  capital intensity of capital goods and of, 14
  export of surplus capital goods in exchange for, 142
  necessities and non-essentials in, 145–8
  turnover tax on, in socialist economy, 5

consumption, 3, 4, 8, 9
  at constant growth rate, 15
  foreign credits and growth rate of, 160
  growth rate and: in mixed economy, 148, 149, 150; in short term and long term, 16, 28–30, 33, 42, 121, 132
  increase of: when growth rate is increased by raising capital–output ratio, 64–6, 69, 70n, 71, 74, 75, 76; when growth rate is increased by reducing life span of capital equipment, 78, 80–2
  optimum capital intensity and life span of capital equipment without sacrifice of, 82–4
  plus productive accumulation, equals national income, 8, 10
  relative share of, in national income, 16, 28–9, 30
  shift to investment from, 14

currency raw materials, sold in foreign trade, 136, 137–9

decision curve, *see* government decision curve

demand
  effective, 12
  income elasticity of, 121

depreciation
  in calculating national income, 1–2, 4
  parameter of, 11, 59, 60, 77, 80; decreasing, 28n, 63n; increasing, 51, 78–9, 80, 81

development, economic
  foreign trade and production technology in solving problem of directions of, 123

problems of financing, in mixed economy, 145–61

Dobb, M., 85, 88, 93, 94, 95

efficiency of investment, coefficient of, 127
  see also under investment

Egypt, big business in, 165

employment
  decreasing: with constant capital–output ratio, 13; with increased labour intensity, 23
  distribution of, between sectors of economy, 9
  full: assumed, 24; level of investment to obtain, 122
  increased rate of, increases growth rate, 27, 28
  increasing *pari passu* with consumption, gives constant real wages, 33, 108
  rate of growth of labour supply and of, 24
  in 'recasting' for lessened capital intensity, 97, 98, 100
  in services, 24

exchange, achieved rate of, 6, 7, 8

exports
  calculation of value of, 6–7, 7–8
  as component of national income, 3, 4
  with increasing growth rate, 42
  obstacles to obtaining most effective pattern of, 122
  production for, 141
  reduction of price of, may not increase total value of, 45
  see also foreign trade

fixed capital, *see* capital equipment

foreign credits, 8
  choice of pattern of, 122, 123
  in financing economic development, 158–61
  to underdeveloped countries: from imperialist countries, 164, 167; from socialist countries, 162, 164

foreign currencies, different possibilities of obtaining, 119

foreign exchange prices, of exports and imports, 6, 9

foreign policy, of Indonesia, 168, 169

Index

foreign trade, 8
  agreeements between countries on, 50
  balancing of, as factor in growth rate, 9, 42–50
  and choice of capital–output ratio, 99–101
  difficulties in, 84
  in financing development in mixed economy, 154–61
  in investment planning, 136–7, 141–2
  and share of investment in national income, 103, 109–11
  various patterns of, and evaluation of investment efficiency, 121, 122, 123
  see also exports, imports
full employment, *see under* employment

'golden rule', 69, 72, 76n
government decision curves, 32, 35–6
  foreign trade and, 47, 48, 49
  with limited labour supply, 41, 49
  when increasing growth rate: by increasing capital–output ratio, 66, 68, 69, 75, 76; by reducing life span of capital equipment, 80–1
government expenditure on housing, health, education: foreign credits and, 161
growth rate of national income
  acceleration of: with labour supply limited, 37–41, 49; with labour supply unlimited, 27–36; by raising capital–output ratio, 61–76; by reducing life span of capital equipment, 77–84
  assumed to be uniform, 17–26
  balancing of foreign trade as factor limiting, 42–50
  basic equations of, 10–16
  investment and, 11, 12–13, 102, 105–6, 148
  in self-sufficient country, 50

hours of work, 74

imports
  calculation of value of, 6–7, 7–8
  deducted from gross national income, 3, 4
  substitution of home-made goods for, 42, 43, 45, 119, 141
  see also foreign trade

income elasticities of demand, 121 146
India, big business in, 165
Indonesia, as non-typical 'intermediate regime', 168–9
industries
  different rates of expansion possible for, 44
  with output lagging behind demand, 50
inflation, 153, 168
inputs into production processes, 1
'intermediate regimes', social and economic aspects of, 162–9
inventories (working capital plus stocks)
  calculation of value of, 6
  as component of national income, 3, 4, 10
  include capital under construction, 4, 14, 34n
  increases in, proportionate to growth rate, 13, 15, 17, 62, 63
investment
  efficiency of: basic problems in theory of, 124–44; production curve and evaluation of, 53n, 112–18; scope of evaluation of, 119–23
  equals volume of capital equipment delivered in given year, 10, 34n
  foreign credits and, 160–1
  increases: when growth rate exceeds rate of supply of necessities, 154; with reduced life span of capital equipment, 78
  increment in national income as function of, 11, 12–13
  minimization of aggregate, for given increase in labour supply, 126–7, 141, 144
  non-productive, 3, 4
  optimal time curve for, 132
  outlay on, in production curve, 52–3
  private, 150
  productive, 3, 4; at constant growth rate, 17, 18; in productive accumulation, 10
  relative share of, in national income, 148
  structure of, 14, 102–11
  variants in, 112, 124–5; choice of, 130–1; may be lacking, 143
investment intensity, 127, 135

Index

peasantry (*cont.*)
  rich, in power, serve interests of big business, 162, and state capitalism, 164
petroleum; exports of, by underdeveloped countries, 154, 155
plan, balanced
  and evaluation of investment efficiency, 120
  from point of view of consumption of materials, 125n
planning, economic
  of investment, 112, 113n, 124–44
  in underdeveloped countries, 163; in Indonesia, 168, 169
  when discrepancy arises between volume of capital investment and consumption, 132
population, rate of increase of, and demand for necessities, 146
prices (in socialist economy)
  of exports, 45
  factory and market, in calculating national income, 4–5
  in reckoning value of exports and imports, 6, 7, 9
  relation between wages and, 12
production
  aim of (non-productive investment and consumption), 4
  in calculating national income, 2
  inputs into, 1
  primary, capital–output ratio in, 14, 104n, 122–3
  variants of methods of, 52, 55, 112
  see also capital intensity of production, labour intensity of production
production curve, 51, 52–3
  and evaluation of efficiency of investment, 112–18
productive accumulation, 4, 8, 9, 10
  rate of (relative share of, in national income), 15, 102; with accelerated growth rate, 15–16, 28–9, 30–3, 35; at constant growth rate, 14–15; foreign trade and, 44–5, 47; with raised capital–output ratio, 62–76 *passim*; with reduced life span of equipment, 78; when increased by whole increase of labour productivity, 86

proletariat, urban and rural: in underdeveloped countries, 165–6

raw materials, 1
  currency and non-currency, 135, 136, 137–40
  economy of, not important in technical progress, 140
  factors limiting output of, 43
  for investment goods, 105
'recasting'
  to obtain higher capital intensity with given life span of capital equipment, 57–60 *passim*, 61–76 *passim*, 85–95 *passim*, 102
  to obtain lower capital intensity, 70, 95–8
recoupment period, 113, 114–15, 116, 118
'rejuvenation', of capital equipment with given capital intensity, 59, 77–82 *passim*, 84
religion, in underdeveloped countries, 167
running costs, distinguished from investment, 11n, 133

'sacrificing the present for the future', 35, 36
scrapping of obsolete equipment, 11, 19n, 28n, 57, 60
  coefficients of, 124, 129, 130, 132, 135n, 140
self-sufficient country, growth rate in, 50
semi-manufactures, in calculation of national income, 1
Sen, A. K., 85, 88, 93, 94, 95
services
  employment in, 24
  not included in national income, 2
spinning, capital intensity of primitive and mechanized, 95
state capitalism, in underdeveloped countries, 163, 164, 167
state interventionism, in developed capitalist countries, 162, 163

taxes
  foreign credits and, 160–1
  in restraint of consumer demand, to finance development in mixed economy, 145, 148, 150, 152, 153, 158

Index

technical progress
  economy of materials in, 140
  labour productivity depends on, 17, 24, 35, 44, 48, 72
  obsolescence resulting from, 133
  types of: discouraging capital intensity, 54, 55–6; encouraging capital intensity, 54–5, 56, 58, 72–6; neutral, 54, 56–8, 61, 90, 97n; uniform, 53
techniques: choice of, and evaluation of investment efficiency, 120–1, 122
technological factors
  in degree of utilization of equipment, 12
  limiting growth rate in particular industries, 43–4, 45, 50, 122, 123
terms of trade, 6–7, 8
trade agreements, to eliminate uncertainty about foreign trade, 50
transformation of capital equipment (combination of 'recasting' and 'rejuvenation'), 82–4
transition period, in increasing rate of productive accumulation while keeping real wages stable, 33, 34, 37, 46, 47, 70n, 86, 102
  lengthening of, 108
turnover, aggregate, 1
turnover tax, on consumption goods in socialist economy, 5

uncertainty about foreign trade, and choice of growth rate, 49–50
underdeveloped countries
  capital intensity in, 95
  social and economic aspects of regimes in, 162–8
  supply of necessities in, 150–1
unemployment, 48, 87
  in underdeveloped countries, 166, 167
United States, foreign aid from, 167

values
  of national income, 5–8
  real: of exports and imports, 7; measurement of changes in, 2

wages
  real: choice of capital–output ratio and, 91, 93, 98; during increases in growth rate, 33, 34, 37, 46, 47, 70n, 108; highest growth rate possible without reducing, 86, 95; when growth rate exceeds rate of supply of necessities, 154
  relation between prices and, in socialist economy, 12
white-collar workers, in underdeveloped countries, 165